Just Transitions

For Geneviève and Aimée: love

Just Transitions

Advancing Environmental and Social Justice

Éloi Laurent

Senior Economist, OFCE-Sciences Po, Professor, Ponts Paris Tech, France and Visiting Professor, Stanford University, USA

Edward Elgar PUBLISHING

Cheltenham, UK • Northampton, MA, USA

Published by
Edward Elgar Publishing Limited
The Lypiatts
15 Lansdown Road
Cheltenham
Glos GL50 2JA
UK

Edward Elgar Publishing, Inc.
William Pratt House
9 Dewey Court
Northampton
Massachusetts 01060
USA

A catalogue record for this book
is available from the British Library

Library of Congress Control Number: 2024946599

This book is available electronically in the **Elgar**online
Sociology, Social Policy and Education subject collection
https://doi.org/10.4337/9781035318414

MIX
Paper | Supporting responsible forestry
FSC® C013604

ISBN 978 1 0353 1840 7 (cased)
ISBN 978 1 0353 1841 4 (eBook)

Printed and bound by CPI Group (UK) Ltd, Croydon, CR0 4YY

Contents

Figures

Tables

Boxes

1. Introduction: Justifying transitions

WHAT ARE JUST TRANSITIONS?

All meaningful conversations among humans that relate to change, reform, and progress eventually center around a robust debate about the principles of justice the people involved want to see upheld and the institutions and policies capable of sustaining them. This is especially true of the titanic change in attitudes and behaviors required to mitigate, stabilize and hopefully reverse the ongoing collapse of the biosphere that is often referred to as the "ecological" or "environmental" transition.

Transitions have a bad name. British activist Rob Hopkins, who was arguably one of the first to introduce the word "transition" into the environmental lexicon (while promoting his "transition towns" project), claims to have chosen the most neutral expression so that reluctant consumers and businesses would not be frightened by the prospect of hard choices, conflicts, and sacrifices entailed by transition policies (Hopkins, 2008). Transitions are supposed to be harmless or at least smooth. In fact, French historian Jean-Baptiste Fressoz convincingly argues that "energy transition" is an expression coined by industrial lobbies in the mid-1970s to prevent the idea of an "energy crisis" from taking hold in Western public debates (Fressoz, 2024). Transitions are supposed to never really happen and remain, forever, ideas for tomorrow.

And yet, this book argues, the concept of transition is actually a very powerful tool to think about what we should be doing in the face of worsening ecological crises and act upon it. Imagining a transition means having to answer three fundamental questions: why is the world we live in not desirable anymore, what other/better world(s) would we want, and how to get from here to there. Moreover, the etymology of the word "transition" distances it from its increasingly pejorative current meaning, that of a gradual, timid, and watered-down process. A transition actually means something completely different: in Latin this word designates a *passage*. The ecological transition can thus be understood as the narrow path that humanity must find in the first half of the 21st century to secure its prosperity going forward.

By embracing the notion of "just transition," this book argues that this passage towards the continuation of the human journey does indeed exist but can only be opened and taken on the condition of sharing the resources, power, and collective intelligence that have made us so prosperous up until this moment in history. This sharing endeavor must be deployed on many fronts at the same time: energy, water, air, soil, climate, biodiversity, health, life itself, and according to various modalities of justice: distribution, redistribution, participation, and recognition. Hence the plural: just *transitions*.

Human transitions are neither magical nor mechanical: they take shape under the pressure of new knowledge, they are driven by irresistible aspirations, starting with the thirst for justice, and they are eventually embodied in robust institutions. Social transitions depend on a triptych bringing together ideas, institutions, and interests: ideas irrigate institutions which shape interests. This is why this book aims at bringing together concepts and frameworks (Part I) and policy designs and emerging institutions (Part II). Its structure reflects the gradual yet continuous progress of the just transition, from philosophical streams to academic fields to public policies eventually embedded in lasting institutions.

The concept of "just transition" is 30 years old: in 1993, US labor leader Tony Mazzocchi[1] foresaw that the jobs, incomes, and pensions of employees in the fossil fuel industries of the United States would soon be subject to strict environmental constraints due to the already looming climate crisis. He thus proposed a way to protect them in the form of a "Superfund" (for contemporary theoretical and policy approaches along those lines, see respectively Eisenberg, 2019[2] and Pollin, 2023[3]). The first written occurence of the term "just transition" can be found in a presentation by Mazzochi's colleague Les Leopold in 1995 at a conference on US great lakes water quality, pointing to a broader view of the intersection of social and ecological issues (Leopold, 1995).

The idea of a just transition has since then gained ground and is now on the agenda of many national and international organizations and governmental institutions (the ILO, the IPCC, the European Union, the federal government of Belgium, the Scottish Government, and many others). Since the COP 26 declaration in December 2021[4] and the launch of the first "Just Energy Transition Partnership" (JETP) agreements, the just transition has even become a core topic of climate negotiations[5].

It has also increased in visibility in the academic literature. Three recent articles published in prominent journals show that the notion of a just transition is gaining ground in academic circles and also evolving in meaning. Rockström, J., Gupta, J., Qin, D. et al. (2023) have extended the literature on "planetary boundaries"[6] to "safe and just Earth system boundaries," adding a justice lens to biophysical metrics. When assessing where humans stand with respect to planetary boundaries regarding climate, the biosphere, fresh water, nutrients, and air pollution at global and sub-global scales, the authors use not just "safe" quantitative thresholds for maintaining Earth system resilience but also three justice criteria (Interspecies justice[7], Intergenerational justice[8] and Intra-generational justice[9]). As a result, some boundaries become more stringent: for climate, while the "safe" limit stands close to 1.5°C, the safe and just limit is set at 1°C, a threshold that human societies have already exceeded.

Gupta et al. (2023) move closer to policymaking by trying to give meaning to the notion of "Earth system justice," which they define as "an equitable sharing of nature's benefits, risks, and related responsibilities among all people in the world, within safe and just Earth system boundaries to provide universal life support." This attempt to move from analysis to policy is especially useful in the perspective of this book (see also Ripple et al 2024).

This policy perspective is even clearer in the third paper, where *Nature*'s editors write: "What the world needs is leaders who can build viable political coalitions to push for truly sustainable — and more equitable — development. Some call this the 'just transition,' from a global economy based on fossil fuels to one that is driven by clean energy. The job of scientists and academics is to be ready with policy options when that day comes. It's not just the right thing to do; it is also our best hope for the future" (Nature, 2023).

While these publications give visibility to just transition approaches[10], it is even more necessary to attempt to stabilize the meaning of the term, focusing on its inner tension between a narrow and broad version (Burke, 2022).

The notion of a just transition was initially understood as a defensive social project aimed at protecting workers in fossil fuel industries from the consequences of climate policies on their jobs and pensions. Its scope was limited in several ways: the people concerned, the domain of ecological crises, and the policy type envisioned to address its consequences. This project found a contemporary echo in the EU with the Silesia/Katowice Declaration in 2018 and the creation of the "Just Transition

Mechanism" of the European Green Deal in 2019; at the global level, it was taken up in the 2015 Paris Agreement (which evokes the "imperatives of a just transition for the active population and the creation of decent and quality jobs in accordance with the development priorities defined at the national").

In this defensive perspective (which is salient in current debates in the United States around the future of coal states like West Virginia), it is the transition policies that must be made just for workers involved in concerned sectors (see Morena et al. 2019 for an overview on climate policies). However, the amplification of ecological shocks (floods, droughts, pandemics, etc.) and their wide-ranging impact call for a broader and positive definition of the just transition in terms of actions and actors, a definition that echoes the origins of the notion (Leopold, 2015). Our ecological crises are now many and systemic: the degradation of ecosystems and biodiversity, the over-consumption of natural resources[11], the pollution and waste of all kinds, etc. and they affect all humans and non-humans on the planet.

This broadening was initiated under the influence of the International Trade Union Confederation (ITUC) and the European Trade Union Confederation (ETUC), which understood the notion of a just transition as an attempt to reconcile climate change mitigation with the reduction of social inequalities. This social-ecological approach is most evident in the 2015 International Labor Organization (ILO) report, which defines "guidelines for a just transition towards environmentally sustainable economies and societies for all" (ILO, 2015). This expanded definition is also used in the Declaration of November 4, 2021, of COP 26 (see Box 1.1), which addresses the traditional themes of supporting workers in the transition toward new jobs characterized by decent work via social dialogue, but embeds them in a new economic strategy that notably involves redefining growth models considered unsustainable on an ecological (overconsumption of resources) and social (exacerbation of inequalities) basis.

Indeed, just transitions should no longer be understood only as social support or financial compensation schemes embedded in policies designed to mitigate ecological crises. Living conditions of humans and non-humans are also transitioning towards a new ecological regime characterized by extreme climate events such as heatwaves, drought, or floods but also pandemics or ecososytems collapse that have profound and socially differentiated impacts. In other words, there are two ongoing transitions: one is the passage towards a new biophysical regime, the other is a passage towards a new social-ecological regime, the second being a response to the first.

This is why this book defines just transitions as *holistic social-ecological strategies to be deployed on all fronts of ecological crises to protect the existence of all humans, as well as non-humans.*

In this broader perspective, a just transition entails (Laurent, 2023)[12]:

- Systematically analyzing ecological shocks (e.g., heat waves and floods) and ecological policies (e.g., energy and/or carbon taxation) from the plural perspective of justice (including the rights of non-human species), with the dual aims of minimizing social inequalities and environmental degradation and maximizing social and environmental co-benefits;
- Giving priority, when designing just transition policies using this analytical framework, to dynamic human well-being informed by justice issues, rather than to the maximization of economic growth. In other words, the just transition should be carried out as part of a "well-being economy," promoting sufficient human development within planetary limits with health and cooperation as cornerstones;
- Designing and implementing these just transition policies democratically by ensuring citizen understanding, support, and participation.

The Just Transition Research Collaborative (2018) has outlined four types of just transition approaches (Status quo; Managerial; Structural; Transformative)[13]. In this respect, the perspective of this book is both structural and transformative: the Anthropocene can be defined as an era where social systems govern natural systems and are affected in return by the dynamics they set in motion to the point of possible collapse. To avoid this collapse, we need to identify socio-economic tipping points to respond to biophysical tipping points. Just transitions policies can help us do *just* that.

WHAT ARE JUST TRANSITIONS POLICIES?

Implementing a just transition policy means articulating social issues and environmental challenges in order to enable simultaneous progress in both areas, either because progress in one field leads mechanically to progress in the other (as in the case of making a home more energy efficient, whereby environmental progress leads to social progress), or because the outcome of social-ecological policy leads by design to parallel progress in both areas (as in the case of a carbon tax whose proceeds benefit the poorest).However, in many cases, considering and designing a just transition policy consists first in recognizing potential conflicts and trade-offs between social and environmental issues in order to subesequently turn them into social-ecological synergies. For instance, in the case of urban air pollution mitigation via low-emission areas without adequate financial support for low-carbon mobility, transition policies can have harmful social and political consequences, widening social inequality and increasing distrust in public authorities. This doesn't mean reconciling ecological and social dimensions is impossible: it means that trade-offs must be acknowledged and turned around (e.g., a low-emission area coupled with sufficient public transportation can improve the health of the most vulnerable people while ensuring the access for all to mobility and adequate standard of living via employment and income).

Transition policies have indeed the power to generate positive environmental co-benefits, such as improved air quality, with positive outcomes in terms of health and well-being. These effects tend to benefit lower-income households and vulnerable people among different social groups and help reduce environmental inequalities. However, measures leading to increased energy prices (e.g., carbon and energy taxes) tend to disproportionately affect lower-income households financially. This can jeopardize the acceptability and effectiveness of such climate policies and, most importantly, lead to an increase in social injustice (Eurofound and EEA, 2021).

More precisely, three types of just transition policies can be designed and implemented:[14]

- Measuring and mitigating the inequalities of the current "non-transition" (the *unjust non-transition*): When ecological crises worsen without a suitable response, the outcome is social inequalities that affect the poorest and most vulnerable primarlity and mostly (this is the social cost of non-transition). These environmental inequalities (such as energy poverty and food insecurity) must be made visible and mitigated;
- Reducing social inequalities to mitigate ecological crises and vice versa: regulation, tax, and transfer policies aimed at reducing inequalities in income or wealth can mitigate environmental degradation, while ecological transition policies can reduce social

inequalities and improve the well-being of the poorest and most vulnerable people (this happens when social-ecological taxation of high emissions luxurious lifestyles occur);
- Designing and then implementing social-ecological policies with citizens, which can—both here and now and in the long term—reduce social inequalities and environmental degradation simultaneously (this is typically the case with democratically decided sufficient housing policies).

These policies are theoretical but also practical: some already exist, if only partially and they convey precious insights in terms of achievements but also limitations of just transition approaches.

WHAT JUST TRANSITIONS INSTITUTIONS ARE EMERGING?

In many corners of the world and at all levels of governance, just transition institutions are emerging, in places where the notion originated initially thirty years ago (trade unions, the workplace, on the issue of energy and climate) but also in many other areas (e.g. local authorities, urban design, biodiversity protection).

The International Labor Organization (ILO) has been instrumental in enlarging and mainstreaming the just transition approach in the last decade. For the ILO, "a just transition means greening the economy in a way that is as fair and inclusive as possible to everyone concerned, creating decent work opportunities and leaving no one behind." (ILO, 2015). In line with both the narrow and broader origins of the just transition, the ILO focuses on employment to embrace a broad vision of the just transition, arguing that it "involves maximizing the social and economic opportunities of climate action, while minimizing and carefully managing any challenges – including through effective social dialogue among all groups impacted, and respect for fundamental labor principles and rights." This dynamic being important "for all countries at all levels of development. It is also important for all economic sectors – by no means limited to energy supply – and in urban and rural areas alike."

The ILO approach has been adopted by the European Trade Union Confederation (ETUC, 2016), which now calls for the adoption of policy measures to operationalize the ILO Guidelines (more recently, the ILO and UNEP issued a joint report detailing the financial means of the just transition)[15] but also been promoted by the ITUC in climate negotiations (Thomas, 2021).

NGOs are also hard at work refining and operationalizing just transitions approaches, such as "Health Care Without Harm," which issued a report shortly after COP27, including a set of original principles for just transition for health (Narayan S., 2023):

1. A Just Transition provides alternative employment and adequate training and assures rate retention and the right to unionize for all workers migrating from polluting industries.
2. A Just Transition protects people's right to health, recognizing that adequate wages and social support, but even more so, a clean environment, are integral to realizing this right.
3. A Just Transition prioritizes people's social, physical, and mental well-being and leaves no one behind.
4. A Just Transition must include a transition in the healthcare sector and invest in low-carbon, climate-resilient public health care infrastructure and services that are anchored by communities and accessible to all.
5. A Just Transition revises the distortions of the fossil fuel industry on culture and history, especially those of racial or ethnic minority peoples, resources the rebuilding of that which was destroyed by its grip, and repairs historical injuries.
6. A Just Transition recognizes the pitfalls of extractive culture, providing means to explore decentralized, diverse, low-carbon, climate-resilient economies centered around population health and healthcare.

National governments are also becoming very active in this area, especially European Union member states, with Spain and Belgium leading the way. In Spain, the Institute for the Just Transition (ITJ)[16] was created on April 28, 2020. Its objective is to identify and adopt measures that guarantee workers and territories affected by the transition to a greener, low-carbon economy, equitable treatment, and solidarity, minimizing the negative impacts on employment and the depopulation of these territories. One of the key policies of the Institute for the Just Transition is the support for areas where mining, coal plants, or nuclear plants have been closed through the "Just Transition Agreements."

In Belgium, the Minister of Climate, Environment, Sustainable Development and Green Deal, Zakia Khattabi launched on May 24, 2022, the "General States for a Just Transition" in line with the Vivaldi Federal Government Agreement concluded on September 30, 2020. Four colleges then went to work: researchers within the High Committee for the Just Transition[17], civil society organized in a Forum[18], a Citizen Agora[19] and federal public administrations[20].

These national efforts develop within the context of a European approach to the just transition embedded in the framework of the European "Green Deal," launched in December 2019. The "Just Transition Mechanism," the "Just Transition Fund"[21] and the "Social Climate Fund" are all new policies designed to combine social and environmental concerns. Under the EU Climate Law, the Commission is to consider the "need to ensure a just and socially fair transition for all" when considering climate targets[22]. A new Commissioner for the Just Transition has been nominated in December 2024 within the European Commission, the executive body of the European Union.

Finally, at the international level, a number of recent initiatives[23] have been developed within the United Nations in the wake of the COP 26 Declaration "Supporting the Conditions for a Just Transition Internationally" (Box 1.1) signed by 30 countries.

BOX 1.1 THE FIVE PRINCIPLES OF AN INTERNATIONAL JUST TRANSITION

1. **Support for workers in the transition to new jobs:** We intend to support communities and regions that are particularly vulnerable to the economic, employment, and social effects of a global transition away from carbon-intensive activity. We will take account the impacts on, and benefits for, all affected by this global transition away from a carbon-intensive economy in developing and emerging economies. We intend for our support to take into account the ILO Guidelines for a Just Transition. We envisage making efforts so that financial flows align with the Paris Agreement temperature goal by promoting pathways consistent with net zero emissions by 2050 and keeping a 1.5°C temperature limit within reach, while also supporting social aspects of the United Nations 2030 Agenda

for Sustainable Development, including the Sustainable Development Goals.

2. **Support and promote social dialogue and stakeholder engagement**: We recognize that the development of effective, nationally coherent, locally driven, and delivered just transition plans within countries is dependent on effective and inclusive social dialogue. We intend to support and promote social dialogue between governments and the representative organizations of workers and employers, including those in secondary industries that are dependent on carbon-intensive industries, as well as other stakeholders, in accordance with, *inter alia* the relevant fundamental rights at work. We also recognize that other key stakeholders need to be engaged to ensure no one is left behind. This support may include strengthening social dialogue through the capacity building of the participants.
3. **Economic Strategies:** We recognize that supporting a just transition from a carbon-intensive economy to a net-zero future not only involves support for clean energy to strengthen the ecological foundations of the economy but also requires enabling frameworks and wider economic and industrial support for workers, enterprises, communities, and countries to create sustainable, competitive economies that foster resource-efficient economic growth, create income and decent jobs, and reduce poverty and inequality. It also requires a sound framework to deal with local ecological impacts of the transition (e.g., contaminated sites). We intend to provide support to developing countries and emerging economies to help them in creating those long-term strategies, ensuring sustainable and inclusive economic recovery and growth, and embedding the creation of decent work and economic diversification.
4. **Local, inclusive, and decent work**: We will aim for new jobs, and transitioning jobs to support the creation of decent, formalized, and sustainable work for people in their local areas. This effort will be coupled with effective support for reskilling and training, as well as adequate, inclusive, and sustainable social protection for those in need. This includes targeting of disadvantaged groups in the local labor market and community, such as those living in poverty, marginalized groups, women, and workers in the informal economy to achieve a transition to formality. In terms of low-carbon investment,

we intend to provide for the inclusion of measures that promote and advance the realization of decent work for all. This includes occupational health and safety in accordance with the ILO Declaration on Social Justice for a Fair Globalization of 2008, and assisting the realization in practice of the principles concerning fundamental rights as reflected in the ILO Declaration on Fundamental Principles and Rights at Work and its Follow-up of 1998. We will work to support skills development and labor policies that support the transition to decent jobs in other sectors and support economic diversification into clean sectors in carbon-dependent regions, while empowering marginalized groups to participate equitably in the transition.

5. **Supply chains**: We recognize that transitions also impact businesses in supply chains and the health, environmental and broader social and economic interests of those economically reliant on those supply chains. We aim to focus on ensuring that existing supply chains, and the new and emerging supply chains required for the clean transition, create decent work for all, including for the most marginalized, and create equitable employment across borders. We intend to advance respect for human rights consistent with the United Nations Universal Declaration of Human Rights, and intend to respect relevant fundamental rights, including the prohibition of slavery, child labor, and forced labor. We urge businesses to ensure their supply chains are free of human rights abuses, including through carrying out corporate due diligence in line with the OECD Guidelines for Multinational Enterprises, the UN Guiding Principles on Business and Human Rights, and the ILO's Tripartite Declaration of Principles concerning Multinational Enterprises and Social Policy. We also intend to consider the wider environmental, health, social, and employment impacts of the operation of global supply chains, including the importance of building climate resilience into supply chains across all industries.
6. **Paris Agreement reporting and Just Transition:** We intend to include information on Just Transition efforts, where relevant, in our national Biennial Transparency Reports in the context of reporting on our policies and measures to achieve our Nationally Determined Contributions.

Source: Supporting the Conditions for a Just Transition Internationally, December 2021. Declaration at the COP 26, November 2021. Signed by the United Kingdom, Austria, Belgium, Canada, Denmark, France, Germany, Ireland, Italy, the Netherlands, New Zealand, Norway, Poland, Spain, Sweden, and the United States.

As these academic and policymaking initiatives make clear, just transition approaches do not need recognition nor visibility anymore; they require clarity and precision. Just transitions approaches are analytical paradigm that allow us to better understand our world, where crisis of inequality and ecological crises feed each other. Environmental sustainability, a condition for economic activity, is closely linked to social justice: environmental challenges are social issues so that it makes environmental sense to mitgate social crises and social sense to mitigate ecological crises. But just transitions approaches are also a means of changing our world for the better: just transitions approaches are social projects where justice is a condition of transitions, both a lever for reforming attitudes and behaviors, and an end, where justice is the ultimate goal.

NOTES

1. Mazzochi (1993).
2. Eisenberg defines the just transition as "the principle of easing the burden decarbonization poses to those who depend on high-carbon industries."
3. Pollin, Robert N. 2023. "Fossil Fuel Industry Phase-Out and Just Transition: Designing Policies to Protect Workers' Living Standards." Journal of Human Development and Capabilities.
4. "Supporting the Conditions for a Just Transition Internationally", which was preceded by the 2018 "Silesia Declaration."
5. The COP 28 "full global stocktake decision text" published on 13 December 2023 mentions the need to "transition away from fossil fuels in energy systems, in a just, orderly and equitable manner" (UNFCCC, 2023).
6. Humans have become biophysical agents. Hence the idea of humanity surpassing "planetary limits," which are quantitative thresholds within which humanity can continue to develop and prosper for generations to come (Steffen et al., 2015). Crossing these limits, as we have done since 1950, amplifies the risk of generating large-scale, abrupt, and/or

irreversible environmental and social changes, which the literature now refers to as "tipping points."

7. "Interspecies justice aims to protect humans, other species, and ecosystems, rejecting human exceptionalism."
8. Intergenerational justice examines relationships and obligations between generations, such as the legacy of greenhouse gas emissions or ecosystem destruction for youth and future generations.
9. "Intragenerational justice includes relationships between present individuals, between states (international), among people of different states (global), and between community members or citizens (communitarian or nationalist)."
10. See also Ripple et al. (2024).
11. On this crisis alone, the numbers are staggering: for two centuries, the human population has been frantically producing an ever-increasing "anthropogenic mass" to meet its needs: cement, sand, gravel, metals, asphalt, bitumen, cardboard, plastic. From 1900 to 2020, all of this human production amounted to 1,154 Gt, and in 2021 it exceeded the total biomass (the weight of all life on Earth, including humans) (Elhacham et al., 2020). Cement alone weighs 9,000 times more than all of humanity, its mass having increased 50-fold since 1940. Each year humans consume around 100 billion tonnes of natural resources, of which only 8 came from recycling.
12. Laurent (2023).
13. "Status quo: approaches that seek to craft transition processes without modifying the current socio-economic system; Managerial: approaches that alter certain rules and arrangements within the existing system; Structural: approaches that use procedural and distributive justice mechanisms to modify aspects of the system; Transformative: approaches that seek to radically overhaul the current system."
14. Laurent, 2023.
15. ILO and UNEP (2023).
16. https://www.transicionjusta.gob.es/es-es/Paginas/Home.aspx
17. Made up of 22 experts specializing in social issues, economics, democratic innovation, and Earth sciences, this High Committee's mission is to share its expertise and advise the government and stakeholders in view of the Conference for a Just Transition. It will also have to produce a special report answering the question, "How to organize and institute the just transition in Belgium?"
18. Around a hundred organized civil society organizations worked on the paths to achieve a sustainable society in 2050. This Forum was organized in several stages. First, a letter inviting each organization to develop its vision and expectations. Then, based on their contributions, two days of work were organized around basic human needs: housing,

transportation, healthcare, and food. A summary report of these different stages and their results was produced.
19. 75 citizens drawn at random will participate in one of the most ambitious citizen assemblies in Belgium. They will have to answer the question, "What conditions must the ecological transition meet to be fair?" Over 4 weekends, they have been invited to make recommendations to make the ecological transition a lever in the fight against inequalities.
20. All colleges have produced a report available at https://www.justtransition.be/en/home
21. Territorial just transition plans define the territories in which the Just Transition Fund will be used. The identification of these territories is carried out through dialogue with the Commission. These plans set out the challenges in each territory, as well as the development needs and objectives to be met by 2030. They identify the types of operations envisaged and specify governance mechanisms. The approval of the territorial just transition plans opens the doors to dedicated financing under the other two pillars of the Just Transition Mechanism.
22. European Climate Law (n 16) art 4(5)(c).
23. See, for instance UNDP (2022), which indicates that "65 of the 170 (38 percent) countries that submitted enhanced/updated NDCs reference just transition (as of 31 October 2022)."

PART I

Streams and Fields

PART I INTRODUCTION

The IPCC (2022) has recently attempted to define social justice and climate justice in clear terms: "*Social justice* comprises just or fair relations within society that seek to address the distribution of wealth, access to resources, opportunity, and support according to principles of justice and fairness. *Climate justice* comprises justice that links development and human rights to achieve a rights-based approach to addressing climate change." Yet, obviously, many principles (i.e., conceptions) of justice co-exist and determine different philosophical streams able to provide a robust basis for such a rights-based approach, connecting, in a broad sense, environmental challenges to social needs and demands.

Philosopher Michael Walzer (Walzer, 1983) spoke in this sense of a "complex equality" in the different "spheres" of justice (economic, political, social, etc.) to which resources, themselves diverse (income, health, etc. and of course the environment), correspond. This plurality of conceptions of justice in the relationship to environmental issues should not be seen as a predicament but rather as an opportunity and even a chance: each stream of environmental justice contributes to the common pool of plural justice.

In this first part, I explore philosophical streams and academic fields that, in my (necessarily selective) view, form the matrix of the many approaches that have crystallized in the just transitions paradigm. This part follows two different typologies: one historical (reviewing philosophical streams in order of appearance), the other analytical (reviewing academic fields according to their core focus).

2. Philosophical streams

THE INDIGENOUS APPROACH

Indigenous environmentalism can certainly claim the title of the oldest environmental justice tradition, but it is also one that was not explicit in the very communities where it was practiced until recently. The assumption that indigenous peoples were the "original environmentalists" or "original conservationists," living in perfect harmony with the environment, is doubly false: it caricatures the natural world as harmonious and indigenous peoples as "noble savages." Far from a nativist romanticism, the blunt historical reality is that the destruction of marine and terrestrial ecosystems has been accompanied by the destruction of the human communities that take best care of them, prompting these communities to react to these destructions.

It is indeed undeniable that contemporary ecological crises bear the mark of brutal colonialism which led to the appropriation and exploitation, past and ongoing, of natural resources by Western powers and the related direct and indirect harm to a number of indigenous communities living off these resources. These dynamics have resulted in the degradation of the social-ecological relationships these communities were able to weave over time within their environment. As Hickel (2021) notes, "economic growth in the North relies on patterns of colonization: the appropriation of atmospheric commons, and the appropriation of Southern resources and labor. In terms of both emissions and resource use, the global ecological crisis is playing out along colonial lines." Conversely, as British historian Richard Grove convincingly shows (1995, 2018), it was in the colonies (especially islands) that the first environmental policies emerged as a reaction to the pressure of economic imperialism and its depredations.

But indigenous environmentalism does exist, with its complexity and limitations, and it has been rediscovered in the contemporary period by ecological thinkers and policymakers who have turned to indigenous peoples for inspiration and good practices (some of which are several thousand years old) in order to reinvent more balanced relationships between contemporary societies and ecosystems. In this respect, "it is increasingly evident that Indigenous Peoples and local communities are essential to maintaining the diversity of life on earth" (ICCA Consortium, 2021; see also IPBES, 2019).

Indigenous environmentalism stems from a fact: indigenous peoples (around 370 million people occupying 20% of the earth's territory belonging to 5,000 different cultures) are more exposed to environmental degradation due to their proximity to natural resources (Indigenous Peoples are affected in at least a third of all documented environmental conflicts worldwide) and their social vulnerability (Scheidel et al. 2023). Natural spaces managed by indigenous peoples under various regimes are confronted with the increasing extraction of resources, and the production of primary, mining, energy, and transport infrastructure, with diverse impacts on the livelihoods and health of local communities. These communities, because they rely heavily on nature and its contributions for their livelihood, health, and existence, will be disproportionately affected by these alterations (IPBES, 2019), but they also serve as global ecological sentinels. Hence the importance of giving indigenous communities their full place in the Convention on Biological Diversity currently being negotiated globally.

In fact, a broader community has come together over the years around the idea of indigenous environmentalism, as evidenced by the two Cochabamba Declarations in 2000 and 2010. In the Bolivian city of Cochabamba, in 2000, a constellation of social movements – ecologists, farmers, inhabitants of urban peripheries, indigenous people – was formed against the privatization of water. This "water war" led, for the first time, to the expulsion of a multinational which had just obtained the local market concession. In 2010, after the failure of the 2009 Copenhagen climate change summit), Cochabamba once again became the place where the indigenous environmental movement gathered and mobilized a broader community. From April 19 to 22, 2010, nearly 35,000 activists, artists, and intellectuals from 142 countries responded to the invitation of Bolivian President Evo Morales and gathered for the People's Summit on Climate Change to formulate and pledge to defend the "rights of the Earth –Mother" (Box 2.1).

BOX 2.1 UNIVERSAL DECLARATION OF THE RIGHTS OF MOTHER EARTH AS PROCLAIMED AT THE WORLD PEOPLE'S CONFERENCE ON CLIMATE CHANGE AND THE RIGHTS OF MOTHER EARTH HELD IN COCHABAMBA, BOLIVIA, ON APRIL 22, 2010

This is a proclamation of the Universal Declaration of the Rights of Mother Earth (ME), which was created at the World People's Conference on Climate Change and the Rights of ME held in Cochabamba, Bolivia, on April 22, 2010.

Article 1 declares that ME is a unique, indivisible, self-regulating living being that sustains and reproduces all beings as an integral part of itself. It has inherent rights just like human and other beings. All other beings have rights which are specific to their type and appropriate for their role and function within their communities. The rights of each being are limited by the rights of other beings, and any conflict between their rights must be resolved in a way that maintains the integrity, balance, and health of ME.

Article 2 declares that ME and all beings have inherent rights to:

- life, existence, respect, and continuity
- maintain their identity and integrity as self-regulating and interrelated beings
- water, clean air, health, and being free from contamination
- not have their genetic structure modified to threaten healthy functioning
- restoration from violations caused by human activities
- a place and to play its role in ME for its harmonious functioning and to live free from maltreatment by human beings.

Article 3. Human beings, all states, and public and private institutions are obliged to:

- recognize and promote the full implementation and enforcement of the rights and obligations in the Declaration
- learn how to live in harmony with ME and ensure that their well-being contributes to its well-being

- defend, protect, and conserve the rights of ME and its integrity, the vital ecological cycles, processes, and balances
- repair damages caused by human violations and hold those responsible accountable for restoring the health of ME
- facilitate the defense of the rights of ME and other beings and prevent human activities from damaging species and ecological cycles
- guarantee peace and eliminate nuclear, chemical, and biological weapons
- promote respect for me and all beings, in accordance with their own cultures
- promote economic systems that are in harmony with me.

Article 4 defines the term 'being' as including ecosystems, natural communities, species, and all other natural entities which exist as part of ME and clarifies that nothing in the Declaration restricts the recognition of other inherent rights of all beings or specified beings.

These matrix declarations have been prolonged until today, for example by the "Red Deal Manifesto" published in 2021 by the Red Nation movement in the United States (in reaction to the "Green Deal" carried out by the Biden administration), under the aegis: "decolonization or extinction." Some contemporary political figures are the embodiment of the indigenous stream of environmental justice, such as the Colombian vice-president, Francia Márquez, whose path has been defined by ecofeminist and indigenous struggles[1].

The Christian approach

In a brief and resounding article published in the journal *Science*, the medievalist historian Lynn White Jr., fully aware of the upheaval of the biosphere, argued that contemporary ecological crises are the fruits of the emergence of an entirely new culture whose deep causes he undertakes to unearth (White Jr., 1967). It appears to him that "Christian axioms" form the basis of this instrumental approach to nature, where all the realities of the physical world are put at the service of humans:

"Christianity," writes White Jr., "is the most anthropocentric religion" the world has known, from which arose, in his view, modern science and technology and their vocation to exploit planetary resources for the benefit of humanity.

Convinced that more science and technology will only aggravate the ecological crises of his time, he therefore calls for an ecological ethics of humility and invokes the figure of Saint Francis of Assisi who "tried to depose man from his monarchy over creation and set up a democracy of all God's creatures." We must follow his example, White Jr. tells us, who at the very end of his article proposes "Francis as a patron saint for ecologists."

Lynn White Jr.'s wish was actually granted by Pope John Paul II in 1979. Moreover, Saint Francis, friend of the poor and author of the Canticle of Brother Sun and Sister Moon (Box 2.2), inspired Pope Francis to write the encyclical Laudato si', published in 2015.

BOX 2.2 CANTICLE OF BROTHER SUN AND SISTER MOON, *ST. FRANCIS OF ASSISI*

Most High, all-powerful, all-good Lord, All praise is Yours, all glory, all honour and all blessings.

To you alone, Most High, do they belong, and no mortal lips are worthy to pronounce Your Name.

Praised be You my Lord with all Your creatures,
especially Sir Brother Sun,
Who is the day through whom You give us light.
And he is beautiful and radiant with great splendour,
Of You Most High, he bears the likeness.
Praised be You, my Lord, through Sister Moon and the stars,
In the heavens you have made them bright, precious and fair.
Praised be You, my Lord, through Brothers Wind and Air,
And fair and stormy, all weather's moods,
by which You cherish all that You have made.
Praised be You my Lord through Sister Water,
So useful, humble, precious and pure.
Praised be You my Lord through Brother Fire,
through whom You light the night and he is beautiful and playful and robust and strong.

Praised be You my Lord through our Sister,
Mother Earth
who sustains and governs us,
producing varied fruits with colored flowers and herbs.
Praise be You my Lord through those who grant pardon for love of You and bear sickness and trial.
Blessed are those who endure in peace, By You Most High, they will be crowned.
Praised be You, my Lord through Sister Death,
from whom no-one living can escape. Woe to those who die in mortal sin! Blessed are they She finds doing Your Will.
No second death can do them harm. Praise and bless my Lord and give Him thanks,
And serve Him with great humility.

This very well-researched text is both a challenge to economic imperialism (condemning, for example, carbon markets) and a call for an integrated vision of social and environmental issues:

> The human environment and the natural environment deteriorate together; we cannot adequately combat environmental degradation unless we attend to causes related to human and social degradation. In fact, the deterioration of the environment and of society affects the most vulnerable people on the planet: "Both everyday experience and scientific research show that the gravest effects of all attacks on the environment are suffered by the poorest"... Today, however, we have to realize that a true ecological approach always becomes a social approach; it must integrate questions of justice in debates on the environment, so as to hear both the cry of the earth and the cry of the poor (Pope Francis, 2015).

THE MARXIAN APPROACH

Against a reductive vision assimilating Karl Marx to industrialism and productivism, Marxist studies took a serious interest in the ecological question in the 1980s, under the impetus of the work carried out in particular by John Bellamy Foster, James O'Connor, Paul Burkett and more recently Kohei Saito. In this light, Marx appears as a key thinker of the social-ecological question, he who writes: "Labor is, in the first place, a process in which both man and Nature participate, and in which man of his own accord starts, regulates, and controls the material re-actions between himself and Nature" (Marx, 1976). There is a close relationship between what Marx designates in the first volume of Capital as the "robbery of the worker" and the "robbery of the soil." In other words, there is a direct and consubstantial link between the alienation of work and the exploitation of nature.

Three major related ideas have emerged or re-emerged from the Marxist matrix over the last two decades to bridge social justice and ecological sustainability: social metabolism as the cause of ecological crises; the predatory nature of capitalism on natural ecosystems; and, finally, "social ecology" as a general framework for understanding how environmental degradation can result from unequal social situations.

The process of "metabolic rift" (or rupture of the social metabolism, a metabolism prescribed by the natural laws of life itself according to Marx) is detailed in the first volume of Capital: "Capitalist production… disturbs the metabolic interaction between man and the earth… All progress in capitalist agriculture is a progress in the art, not only of robbing the worker, but of robbing the soil; all progress in increasing the fertility of the soil for a given time is progress towards ruining the more long-lasting sources of that fertility… Capitalist production, therefore, only develops the technique and the degree of combination of the social process of production by simultaneously undermining the original sources of all wealth—the soil and the worker." (Marx, 1976). It was Foster (1999, 2000) who named this human-nature disconnection "metabolic rift," in reference to Marx's notion of an irreparable rupture in the interdependent process of social metabolism[2].

This metabolic rift is part of a critique of the economic theory of value. As Foster points out, in Marx's critique of political economy, all human production has a real basis (a "material substrate [...] provided by nature without human intervention"), while the labor process is a mediation between man and nature. The commodity fulfills a dual function as natural material and use value, meeting social needs, and as exchange value, generating capitalist surplus value. It is capitalism's exclusive focus on producing for exchange value rather than use value, and its treatment of nature as a free gift, that led Marx to denounce the "robbery" of nature, illustrated in the 19th century by the soil crisis in which essential nutrients from cultivated land were shipped to new urban centers of industrial production, where they contributed to pollution and eventually escaped biospheric cycles.

This perspective extends with the idea that ecological crises are the consequence of a disruption in the exchange of materials between societies and their environment, a disruption which can occur in various historical conditions, but which the capitalist mode of production has greatly accelerated everywhere it took hold. Jason Moore, for instance (Moore, 2015) shows how capitalism induces a way of organizing collective relationships with nature, and of organizing them in the perspective of ever more intensive and extensive exploitation (fossil energies are a notable example, which allow both for the intensification and expansion of capitalism). Hence the concept of "Capitalocene" developed by Moore, understood as a system of power, profit, and re/production propelling humanity into a new era of manufactured ecological crises and breakdowns.

Ecological Marxism enriches the definition of the capitalist system: while capitalism entails a manipulation of economic time according to Fernand Braudel and entails a disjunction between the exercise of work and the ownership of the means of production according to Karl Marx, ecological Marxists add that capitalism entails a disjunction between the exercise of work and the flows of raw materials and natural resources on which it is based.

Murray Bookchin's work around "social ecology" represents the third essential contribution of Marxist studies to the political economy of the environment, undoubtedly more marginal but entirely central to the subject of this book. In a series of books and articles, the first of which was "Ecology and Revolutionary Thought" (Bookchin, 1964), the American thinker and activist forcefully affirmed the central thesis of what he called "social ecology": "all ecological problems have their roots in social problems." Social ecology, as defined by Bookchin, does not incriminate individual human motivations or behaviors, such as the greed to consume or the appetite for profit. Its focal point is the social system and its structures. Because of this focus on institutions rather than individuals, Bookchin managed to uncover new forms of human cooperation, proposing to build "communalism" at the local level (and even a confederation of independent communes instead of the nation-state) against what he perceived as the false alternative of centralized power and laissez-faire (Bookchin, 1993).

ECOFEMINISM

Ecofeminism is an activist movement and academic discipline that highlights the fundamental link between the exploitation of nature and the exploitation of women and denounces a single oppressive ideology at the origin of the domination of both women and the biosphere. As an academic discipline, ecofeminism was founded by Françoise d'Eaubonne in Feminism or Death (d'Eaubonne, 1974), then extended by Carolyn Merchant in The Death of Nature (Merchant, 1980), which deepened the critique of patriarchal double exploitation.

The founding moment of the activist movement is generally thought to be the conference "Women and Life on Earth: Ecofeminism in the Eighties," which was held in Amherst (Massachusetts, United States) in March 1980 to illuminate the interlinkages between feminism, militarism, health, and ecology. The event was followed by the formation of Women's Pentagon Action, a feminist, anti-militarist, and anti-nuclear group, and evolved into a broad activist movement that continued to develop in North America in the 1980s and 1990s.

One of the organizers of the Amherst conference, Ynestra King, explained in clear terms the common belief that animated the participants: "Ecofeminism affirms the particular strength and integrity of each living being. We see the devastation of the earth and its creatures by entrepreneurial warriors, and the threat of nuclear annihilation by military warriors, as feminist concerns. It is the masculinist mentality that deprives us of our right to our own body and our own sexuality, and which depends on multiple systems of domination and state power" (King, 1983).

As the French philosopher Catherine Larrère rightly points out, ecofeminism "develops a new type of attention to environmental issues (linked to health and vulnerability) and calls into question an autonomy of the economy which obscures its double dependence on the home and the terrestrial environment" (Larrère, 2012). This is why, for instance, productive activities (employment, income) must be embedded in reproductive activities (child care, domestic tasks, etc.) on which they actually depend.

Because the concepts of nature and gender are socially constructed, they vary across cultures. Hence, the need for ecofeminism to integrate a plurality of cultural perspectives. Vandana Shiva (1988) thus extends ecofeminism to developing countries and non-Western cultures (in her case, India) to unveil how ecological destruction and the marginalization of women are closely intertwined and, more precisely how rural Indian women feel and perceive environmental degradation and how they have, in turn designed and implemented processes to end the destruction of nature and begin its regeneration. Shiva denounces contemporary economic systems and their inherent environmental destruction, as much as the conception of relationships between humans and ecosystems, which prevails in the West: "Considered from the point of view of the concrete experience of women in the Third World, the modes of thought and action that underpin modern science and development are projects of masculine and Western origin, both historically and ideologically. They are the latest and most brutal expression of a patriarchal ideology that threatens to annihilate nature and the entire human species" (Shiva, 1988).

In this line of thought, the pioneering work of Bina Agarwal on gender inequality as a cause of environmental dysfunction is a fundamental reference in contemporary ecofeminism (Agarwal, 2016). In one of her numerous field studies (Agarwal, 2009), Agarwal demonstrates that the proportion of women within the governing bodies of forest conservation organizations in India and Nepal determines, all things being equal, the state of forests in both regions (the beneficial impact of the presence of women being attributable in particular to the contributions of women in respecting existing rules but also to their cooperative practices and their knowledge of plant species and methods of extracting products from forests).

THE MULTI-SPECIES APPROACH

Some 50,000 species of animals and plants are used today to serve human needs[3]. Our relationship with other living beings that populate the Biosphere is turning into relentless exploitation. In addition to direct predation[4], humans have taken the lead of an army of machine-animals whose utilitarian use destroys the rest of life (through deforestation, climate crisis fueled by methane emissions from cattle herds, pollution of soils and waterways caused by agricultural pollution, etc.). Humans and their machine-animals now represent 96% of wild terrestrial mammals[5].

Against this backdrop, the multi-species justice approach[6] aims at a "reconfiguration of justice – including broadening conceptions of the subject of justice and the means and processes of recognition and misrecognition" (Celermajer et al. 2020). At the confluence of different currents of academic literature, multi-species justice affirms that animals, plants, and more generally non-human species have agency and rights and that a transition based on justice principles cannot be solely driven by human considerations.

An important step in recognizing the continuity between humans and non-humans has been taken with the development of the "One-Health" approach in the early 2000s and later with the "Planetary Health" approach[7].

The so-called "One Health" approach considers human health, animal health, plant health, and environmental health as complementary and interdependent and has recently been acknowledged at the highest international level by the 2022 COP 15 Framework (Kunming-Montreal Global biodiversity framework)[8]:

> *One Health is an integrated, unifying approach that aims to sustainably balance and optimize the health of people, animals and ecosystems.*
>
> *It recognizes the health of humans, domestic and wild animals, plants, and the wider environment (including ecosystems) are closely linked and inter-dependent.*
>
> *The approach mobilizes multiple sectors, disciplines and communities at varying levels of society to work together to foster well-being and tackle threats to health and ecosystems, while addressing the collective need for clean water, energy and air, safe and nutritious food, taking action on climate change, and contributing to sustainable development.*[9]

NOTES

1. A path narrated in the documentary IGUALADA, directed by Juan Mejia and released in 2024.
2. The notion of metabolism (Stoffwechsel in German or "material exchange") refers to the idea of work understood as mediation in a broader system of physical exchanges that imposes limits on it and of which it inevitably remains a part.
3. IPBES (2022).
4. Which affects a third of all vertebrates or 10,000 species (Darimont, Cooke, Bourbonnais et al. 2023).
5. Since the emergence of humans on Earth about 7 million years ago, the number of wild terrestrial mammals (tigers, otters, pandas) has fallen by 85%, so that two-thirds of all remaining mammals are now livestock (especially cattle, poultry, and pigs), see Bar-On, Phillips, and Milo (2018).
6. Celermajer et al. 2020.

7. "Planetary health" has been defined as "the health of human civilization and the state of natural systems on which it depends" (Horton et al. 2015).
8. The framework (CBD, 2022) acknowledges the interlinkages between biodiversity and health and is to be implemented with consideration of the One Health Approach, among other holistic approaches that are based on science, mobilize multiple sectors, disciplines, and communities to work together, and aim to sustainably balance and optimize the health of people, animals, plants, and ecosystems, recognizing the need for equitable access to tools and technologies, including medicines, vaccines, and other health products related to biodiversity, while highlighting the urgent need to reduce pressures on biodiversity and decrease environmental degradation to reduce risks to health, and, as appropriate, develop practical access and benefit-sharing arrangements.
9. One Health High-Level Expert Panel (OHHLEP), Adisasmito WB, Almuhairi S, Behravesh CB, Bilivogui P, et al. (2022).

3. Academic fields

Stemming from these rich and diverse philosophical streams, three main political economy academic frameworks have been assembled in the last three decades that together form the matrix of the just transition paradigm.

- The inequality-unsustainability nexus identified by US economist James Boyce allows us to understand the intertwining of social and ecological dynamics connected by inequality.
- Because of these imbricated logics, winners and losers of environmental degradations enter into a host of conflicts all over the world, as economic historian Joan Martinez-Alier has shown throughout his work.
- Because of these conflicts, social-ecological governance is necessary and, when grounded in robust institutions, proves highly beneficial, as political scientist and economist Elinor Ostrom has shown.

Let's examine, in this logical order, each of these academic frameworks.

JAMES BOYCE AND THE INEQUALITY-UNSUSTAINABILITY NEXUS

The two major crises at the beginning of the 21st century, the inequality crisis and the ecological crisis, need to be studied jointly to be fully understood and possibly mitigated. This intersection of ecological and social fields was delineated thirty years ago by James Boyce with these words: "Economic activities that degrade the environment generally create winners and losers. Without the winners – the people who benefit from this degradation, or at least who think so – these destructive activities would not take place. Without the losers – the people who bear the cost of this degradation – this destruction would not matter in terms of human well-being." (Boyce, 1994).

Within this framework, inequality appears as much a cause than a consequence of the destruction of our environment: social inequalities catalyze ecological crises, which in turn accelerate social inequalities. Greta Thunberg, an environmental activist then aged 15, said it with her words at COP 24 on December 15, 2018: "Our biosphere is being sacrificed so that the rich in countries like mine can live in luxury. It is the suffering of the many that is the price of the abundance of the few."

Boyce has shed light on the driving forces of what he would refer to later as the "political economy of the environment" (Boyce, 2002). The novelty of Boyce's approach is to study both current environmental challenges (such as climate change or air pollution) and current economic problems (such as uneven development and neoliberal globalization) through the prism of power inequalities and their corollary, income. Boyce distinguishes between five different dimensions of power: purchasing power, decision-making power, agenda-setting power, value power, and event-related power. Purchasing power is classically defined as the ability to purchase goods and services produced in the economy. Decision-making power refers to the ability to decide on more or fewer environmental regulations. The distribution of agenda power refers to the ability to determine which topics receive attention from media and policymakers, while value power affects how people's values and beliefs are shaped and changed by public debate. Finally, event power refers to the ability to influence events that form the framework within which people must then make decisions (Laurent and Zwickl, 2021).

Within this framework, empirical research is able to identify winners and losers from environmentally degrading activities, as well as the dynamics between the two groups, revealing how winners are able to continue their activities while imposing their negative consequences on the losers.

For instance, researchers at the Political Economy Research Institute (PERI) at the University of Massachusetts Amherst were able to create several indices of pollution connecting polluters on the one hand and "pollutees," among whom ethnic minorities and socially vulnerable groups (Box 3.1).

BOX 3.1 CORPORATE TOXICS

The Greenhouse Suppliers 100 ranks companies by their 2020 supply of products that result in greenhouse gas emissions when released, combusted, or oxidized. The top four companies are petroleum refiners: Marathon Petroleum, Phillips 66, Valero Energy, and Exxon Mobil. Marathon Petroleum and Phillips 66 also extract natural gas. The top four each produced fossil fuels that resulted in at least 280 million metric tons of CO2-equivalent emissions. Fifth-ranked Peabody Energy is on the list because of coal mining. Rounding out the top 10 are Enterprise Products Partners, Chevron, BP, Arch Resources, and Shell PLC.

The Greenhouse 100 ranks companies by 2020 direct emissions of greenhouse gases from facilities. The top three companies are Vistra Energy, Duke Energy, and Southern Company, continuing a four-year period in which these were in the top three. Each released more than 75 million metric tons of CO2-equivalent emissions. Together, these three companies released 4 percent of all US greenhouse gas emissions from all sources, including non-energy sources. The rest of the top 10 in the Greenhouse 100 are Berkshire Hathaway, American Electric Power, Energy Capital Partners, NextEra Energy, Xcel Energy, and Exxon Mobil, with the US government ranked 9th. The top company whose direct emissions are not dominated by electric power plants is Exxon Mobil at rank 10. Among the top 10, Energy Capital Partners has the highest weighted share of minorities living within 10 miles of its facilities.

The Toxic 100 Air Polluters report indicates that the top 10 companies, according to the US EPA's estimate of the 2020 total potential chronic human health risk from toxic chemical air pollutants, are LyondellBasell, BASF, Becton Dickinson, Salzgitter, Huntsman, Dow Inc, Canopus International, Celanese, Berkshire Hathaway, and NOV Inc. Five of these companies are in the top 10 almost entirely because of chromium or ethylene oxide emissions from one facility. EPA assesses not just how many pounds of pollutants are released, but which pollutants are the most toxic and who is exposed. The index includes environmental justice indicators: for example, while minorities make up just under 40 percent of the US population, they bear 68 percent of the air-toxics risk from facilities owned by LyondellBasell.

The Toxic 100 Water Polluters ranks the pounds of toxics released into surface water or sent to water treatment systems, adjusted for chemical toxicity, based on EPA data. Northrop Grumman, LyondellBasell, NextEra Industries, Dow Inc., and Cargill top the Toxic 100 Water for 2020. The Toxic 100 Water includes Environmental Justice indicators: for example, minorities bear 63% of the toxic hazard from water releases and transfers to water treatment facilities by Dow Inc.

Source: PERI's Corporate Toxics Information Project on the web at http://toxic100.org

JOAN MARTINEZ-ALIER AND SOCIAL-ECOLOGICAL CONFLICTS

Joan Martinez-Alier, professor of economics and economic history at the University of Barcelona, is the founder of the most prominent school of ecological economics today in the world[1]. In his major book, *The Environmentalism of the Poor*, Joan Martinez-Alier (2002) argues that the cost of extraction, transport, and consumption of natural resources, activities which have been intensifying on the surface of the planet since the 1940s and 1950s and which lead to considerable pollution and waste, is primarily borne by the poorest and most vulnerable, of whom indigenous communities form the front line. This is why there is, and has been for a long time, a "spontaneous environmentalism of the poor." While indigenous represent[2] about 6.2% of the world's population, "they steward about a quarter of the world's terrestrial surface" and "are involved in at least 34% of documented environmental conflicts over extractive and industrial development projects."

According to Martinez-Alier, this reality is coupled with a conviction-based, activist environmentalism, which intends to remove natural resources from the commercial sphere and its set of values: the poor, by demanding sustainable access to resources and services of the environment against capital and/or the State, at the same time contribute to their conservation, argues Martinez-Alier. From the tension between the ecological world and the economic world, mediated by the social question, many "ecological-distributive conflicts" have resulted (from Tambo Grande in Peru to Coega in South Africa) in which indigenous communities defend plural values of natural resources against their sole market and monetary value here and now. These "ecological distribution conflicts"[3] arise because capitalists are constantly in search of sources of energy, materials, and waste disposal. And yet, they are understudied: 75% of existing studies focus on the instrumental value of ecosystems and nature biodiversity with only 20% focused on intrinsic values and

6% on relational values (IPBES, 2022). Hence the need to document empirically "ecological-distributive conflicts."

This is why Martinez-Alier engaged in the co-creation of the Global Atlas of Environmental Justice or EJAtlas, a resource available online[4] collecting socio-environmental conflicts since 2011. The EJAtlas conceptualizes "socio-environmental conflicts" or "ecological distribution conflicts" as "the result of the unfair distribution of environmental 'goods' – i.e., clean water and air, as well as access to fertile land – and 'bads' – i.e., exposure to pollution, as well as risks and threats to health, livelihoods, and social and cultural identities"[5]. The EJAtlas shows, for instance that the most "conflictive commodities" are land and water, but also Rare Earths and Waste, and that "more than three-fourths of these conflicts are caused by mining, fossil fuels, dam projects, and the agriculture, forestry, fisheries, and livestock (AFFL) sector" (Arnim Scheidel et al., 2023).

The many mobilizations globally lead to real ecological progress: for instance, the protest and struggle movements of North American indigenous communities against giant pipeline projects (like the Keystone XXL) have made it possible in recent years to avoid the emission of 5.5 billion tonnes of CO2.

From Martinez-Alier's line of work results a counter-intuitive truth: ecology is not a luxury but a necessity; it is not the prerogative of a wealthy class that has sublimated its material needs but the condition for the survival of disadvantaged populations on all continents. The poor are the first victims of environmental degradation: they are ecological sentinels who alert us to the reality of the ongoing crises that they are the first to feel due to their social vulnerability, but which concern us and will ultimately affect us all. For instance, the inhabitants of the Pacific Islands alert us to the rapid rise of seas and oceans under the effect of climate change, which affects us more slowly but just as surely. As David Schlosberg and David Carruthers argue: "Threats to indigenous peoples – their rights, their lands, and their cultures – have been a powerful catalyst for mobilization, as indigenous communities fight against corporations, governments, policies, and other forces that threaten to fragment them, displace them, assimilate them, or lead them to cultural disintegration" (Schlosberg and Carruthers, 2010). In short, Martinez-Alier shows us that the world is not just in crisis but, more importantly, in struggle.

ELINOR OSTROM AND SOCIAL-ECOLOGICAL GOVERNANCE

"I was born in Los Angeles, California, on August 7, 1933, and grew up during the Great Depression. Fortunately, our house had a large backyard that we filled with a vegetable garden and fruit trees. I learned how to grow vegetables and how to can apricots and peaches during the heat of summer." (Ostrom, 2024). With these words, Ostrom described the first years of her life, subtly mixing social challenges and natural resources.

Of modest means, Ostrom was the first in her family to go to university and decided at first not to undertake unaffordable doctoral studies. Confronted with the ordinary sexism of the 1950s United States, she managed to rise in the hierarchy of a local company which, according to her, "had never hired a woman for any position other than secretary". She then decided to resume her graduate studies, not without difficulty[6].

One of the very first articles published in the journal which would for a long time become the reference in the economic discipline, the *American Economic Review*, was written by a woman and focused on environmental issues. Katharine Coman set out in 1911 to examine the problems of collective action linked to irrigation in the American West, problems of utmost relevance today and which would occupy Ostrom during her doctorate devoted to the study of water management in California. Ostrom gradually broadened her topic to map out and then systematically analyze the institutions that allow (or did not allow) sustainable exploitation of natural resources. How do lobster fishermen in Maine fairly distribute fishing rights while taking care of their common resource, which is the guarantee of their standard of living? How do communities in Nepal sustainably exploit forest resources? How do communities in Spain manage water scarcity? These were the concrete issues Ostrom wanted to clarify.

Biologist Garrett Hardin intended to show in 1968 that individuals, caving to their personal interests, would therefore march blindly toward collective ruin, and that the intervention of a central external authority was the only force able to produce and impose standards to curb these self-destructive behaviors and safeguard common prosperity (Hardin, 1968). Ostrom's work (Ostrom, 1990) will demonstrate, conversely, that the institutions which allow the preservation of resources through cooperation are generated by local communities themselves, in what amounts to a double invalidation of Hardin's hypothesis: cooperation is possible, and it is self-determined.

Ostrom starts from a fundamental discovery made in the laboratory by means of "games": individuals cooperate much more than standard theory presupposes. She would verify this intuition, on the ground, across the world: in hundreds of carefully documented cases, humans manage to avoid the "tragedy of the commons" by constructing collective rules whose pillars are reciprocity, trust, and justice. Whether it is rivers that must be preserved from pollution, forests that must be exploited reasonably while maintaining their carrying capacity[7], fish that must be caught in moderation to allow them to reproduce, from Switzerland to Japan, Spanish irrigation systems to Nepalese irrigation systems, humans are showing themselves capable of cooperating to preserve, conserve and prosper. Based on her field observations, Ostrom endeavors to define the main principles, eleven in number, of sustainable management of common resources (Ostrom, 2010)[8].

Elinor Ostrom has sought to systematically understand what she calls "complex social-ecological systems" like these (Ostrom, 2009). Such systems can be broken down into four essential elements: resource systems, resource units, users, and governance systems. Ostrom takes the example of a protected park where there are forests, animal and plant species, and water resources, which include resource systems (the park contains forested areas, flora, fauna, and fauna, systems water); resource units (e.g., trees, shrubs, park plants, different types of wildlife, water volume, and flow); users (those who use park resources for recreational, subsistence, or commercial purposes); and finally, the governance systems (a national government, non-governmental organizations possibly involved in the management of the park, the rules for the use and exploitation of resources). Ostrom then defines two additional notions: interactions between users (information sharing, deliberation processes, etc.) and their results (economic and ecological results). In this dynamic and complex framework, where ecology, economics, and society combine and where natural and physical sciences, economic discipline, and political science are articulated, Ostrom manages to analyze and design new ways of governing common goods.

Laboratory experiments, field work, empirical case studies, theoretical frameworks: Ostrom juggled, hard at work in her workshop at Indiana University, with varied methods and approaches, at the frontier of political science, social psychology, and environmental studies to profoundly renew economic discipline and convey to us a tremendous lesson of hope for the continuation of the human adventure on the planet. Yes, human collective intelligence is boundless, as long as humans understand that the technology of the future in which we excel is social innovation.

This is how she summarizes the meaning of her work: "Designing institutions to force (or nudge) entirely self-interested individuals to achieve better outcomes has been the major goal posited by policy analysts for governments to accomplish for much of the past half-century. Extensive empirical research leads me to argue that instead, a core goal of public policy should be to facilitate the development of institutions that bring out the best in humans. We need to ask how diverse polycentric institutions help or hinder the innovativeness, learning, adapting, trustworthiness, and levels of cooperation of participants, and the achievement of more effective, equitable, and sustainable outcomes at multiple scales." (Ostrom, 2010).

NOTES

1. Villamayor-Tomas and Roldan Muradia, 2023.
2. Arnim Scheidel et al. (2023).
3. Martinez-Alier, J., 2002; Martinez-Alier and M. O'Connor, 1999.
4. https://ejatlas.org/
5. Del Bene and Ávila (2023).
6. Here is her cautionary tale of her attempt to pursue a doctorate in economics: "My initial discussions with the Economics Department at UCLA about obtaining a Ph.D. in Economics were, however, pretty discouraging. I had not taken mathematics as an undergraduate primarily because I had been advised as a girl against taking any courses beyond algebra and geometry in high school. While the Economics Department encouraged me to take an outside minor in economics for my Ph.D., they discouraged any further thinking about doing a Ph.D. in economics. Political Science at that time was also skeptical about admitting any women to their Ph.D. program as they feared that only a city college would employ a woman with a Ph.D. That was not a good placement for building the reputation of the UCLA department. I was, however, admitted in a class of 40 students with three other women. We were told after we began our program that the faculty had a very heated meeting in which they criticized the Departmental Committee for admitting any women and offering them assistantships." (Ostrom, 2024).
7. The operational carrying capacity (OCC) of a forest can be defined as "the biomass that can be harvested annually without affecting the resource renewability" (Martire et al., 2015).
8. These rules are: "Clear and locally understood boundaries between legitimate users and nonusers are present; clear boundaries that separate a

specific common-pool resource from a larger social-ecological system are present; appropriation and provision rules are congruent with local social and environmental conditions; appropriation rules are congruent with provision rules; the distribution of costs is proportional to the distribution of benefits; most individuals affected by a resource regime are authorized to participate in making and modifying its rules; individuals who are accountable to or are the users monitor the appropriation and provision levels of the users; individuals who are accountable to or are the users monitor the condition of the resource; sanctions for rule violations start very low but become stronger if a user repeatedly violates a rule; rapid, low-cost, local arenas exist for resolving conflicts among users or with officials; the rights of local users to make their own rules are recognized by the government; when a common-pool resource is closely connected to a larger social-ecological system, governance activities are organized in multiple nested layers." (Ostrom, 2010).

PART II

Policy designs, tools and institutions

PART II INTRODUCTION

Philosophical streams of environmental justice have irrigated social-ecological academic fields, whose cultivation gradually leads to the emergence of just transitions institutions, i.e., robust forms of social cooperation, whether formal (law, State, Constitution, etc.) or informal (codes of conduct, cultural norms, imagination, etc.), which govern human societies over time. The early stages of these institutions are just transitions policies, i.e., ideas that can be translated into action (or actionable ideas), stemming from designs and using tools.

4. Rethinking justice narratives, inequality and public policy

In order to reimagine public policy at the crossroads of social justice and environmental sustainability—that is to design and implement just transition policies—it is useful to keep in mind two key insights brought about by recent surveys. The first insight is that environmental policy will be opposed and resisted if it is perceived as socially unfair: this is the obvious conclusion many observers rightly drew from the "Yellow vests" movement that rocked France in 2018–2019 and the conclusion of many studies since (see for instance Kukowski and Garnett, 2023). The second insight is that, conversely, majorities of people in very different countries around the world are willing to support environmental policies provided they are perceived as fair (Dechezleprêtre et al., 2022b).

The "Yellow Vest" crisis is a major event in contemporary France and cannot be fully understood without placing it in its social and political context. The social context is a sharp rise in energy poverty in the country: nearly 3.8 million French households (i.e. 8 million people) are considered to be in a situation of energy poverty (i.e. 15% of the French population), including more than 40% of households in the first income quartile (the bottom 20% of the income distribution). Between February 2016 and October 2018, the price of gasoline increased in France by 26% and that of diesel by 50%. The tax component of the price of fuel being close to 60%, the protest against the price of fuel transformed into a protest against unfair taxation. This is where the political context comes into play: as the energy crisis was unfolding, a reduction in taxes for the wealthiest was being implemented by the Macron government (suppression of the solidarity tax on wealth – ISF – and introduction of a flat-rate tax on capital income). Recent studies have convincingly shown that the "Yellow Vests" movement was neither predominantly climate skeptic nor even anti-environmental[1]. Nor do its members appear to be opposed to the principle of carbon taxes: they are above all opposed to the carbon tax proposed by the French government (Mehleb et al., 2021).

At the heart of the social-ecological revolt of the Yellow Vests thus stood a demand for social and fiscal fairness. In view of the poorly designed French carbon tax, this demand appeared legitimate, as the increase in the French carbon tax from 44 to 55 euros per tonne reinforced injustice by increasing vertical inequalities, horizontal inequalities, and energy poverty (Berry and Laurent, 2019). In fact, the increase in the carbon tax affected the 1st income decile (the poorest 10%) much more, the impact for this social group being 1.5 times greater than the average impact in the population and 2.6 times greater than the impact on the richest 10%. Similarly, the impact on the first six deciles of the income distribution was greater than the average impact, while it was lower for the top four deciles. Finally, based on energy poverty indicators, the increase in the carbon tax from 44.60 euros/tCO2 to 55 euros/tCO2 would have pushed 110,000 additional households into energy poverty (due to housing), i.e. an increase of 2.3% compared to the situation without an increase in the carbon tax, and 47,000 additional households into energy poverty (due to transport), i.e. an increase of 2% compared to the situation without an increase in the carbon tax.

The main measure decided by the government in the face of the "Yellow Vest" revolt, the freezing of the carbon tax at 44 euros per tonne, did not solve those pressing inequalities: if the increase in the carbon tax from 44 to 55 euros per tonne (i.e. 11 euros increase) was indeed frozen in 2019 under social pressure (at the same time as various measures in favor of purchasing power were taken), French citizens continue to pay a tax of 44 euros per ton on carbon without social compensation, which means that a tax injustice four times greater than that which was denounced and fought at the end of 2018 is perpetuated.

And, yet, there is no inevitability in this inequality: a fair carbon tax in France could be implemented in the short term using social and residential criteria (Laurent and Berry, 2019)[2] and would probably be widely accepted. Many countries and localities (such as the Nordic countries but also Indonesia) have indeed successfully introduced such compensations, for instance the province of British Columbia, where a carbon tax was rejected by 43% of its residents when it was introduced without social compensations in 2008 and is now supported by a large majority (support grew when compensations were introduced)[3]. A recent study shows that the methods of redistribution of this tax are decisive for its acceptance: a fair carbon tax is supported by a large majority of the French population provided its revenues are used to finance green investments and/or financial compensation for vulnerable households (Dechezleprêtre et al., 2022a).

What this means is that just transition policies are feasible and acceptable but must be grounded in robust justice principles and narratives.

RETHINKING JUSTICE NARRATIVES

Public policy can draw from a vast toolbox from which imagination is often forgotten. And yet, the ability to influence attitudes that can modify behavior – in other words to alter the value system of individuals and groups to initiate actions deemed desirable – is an essential lever that relies on the power of desire rather than reason.

An international study[4] confirms that "simply making people more worried about climate change is not an effective strategy to foster policy support". The survey, carried out with more than 40,000 respondents in 20 countries representing 72% of global CO2 emissions, provides precious insights as to how a just transition policy can become reality (Dechezleprêtre A. et al., 2022b). The authors show that in all countries, support for climate policies depends on three key factors: the perceived effectiveness of policies in reducing emissions, their perceived distributive effects on low-income households (concerns of inequality) and their own household's gains and losses. The key to political support for environmental policies is to explain "how policies work and who can benefit from them, [which] is essential to foster political support". Thus, when a tax of 45 euros per ton on fossil fuels is submitted to respondents (an ecologically effective measure to combat climate change but also a potentially socially unjust one as we have seen with the yellow vests episode), it does not receive a majority anywhere. But when it is accompanied by compensation measures for the poorest households, a majority supports it (sometimes significantly above 50%, in five out of eight major OECD economies). The authors conclude that "specific policies proposed need to be progressive and that citizens need to be made aware of that".

But an even more interesting insight is the comparison between different kinds of justice narrative and their power to generate public support. When presented with different types of measures to mitigate climate change (i.e. policy options), respondents prioritize public revenues being used to fund green infrastructure and low-carbon technologies[5] and, in second place, favor revenues from carbon taxation being redistributed to households with lower incomes or households strongly affected by the carbon tax (for example in rural areas), via lower income taxes or cash transfers.

At the European level, and more precisely in the European Union, a recent Eurobarometer survey provides converging insights (European Commission, 2023a) in showing that Europeans support social justice as well as the green transition (European Commission, 2023b) but feel this green transition is and might be socially unfair (88% of EU citizens support the goal of "a green transition that leaves no one behind" but only 46% of Europeans are currently confident that by 2050 sustainable energy, products and services will be affordable for everyone, including poorer people")[6]. The risk of social inequalities generated by the transition is perceived as high, especially for those who are obliged to travel by car (70% see a risk of inequality); What is more, more than half of Europeans (55%) fear that the energy transition will further fragment society[7].

The study moreover shows that people respond very differently to different measures proposed to them to sustain a just transition. When asked to rank five measures to mitigate climate change[8], almost nine in ten (89%) favor subsidising people to help make their homes more energy efficient, the same proportion (89%) support increasing their country's investments in public transport infrastructure and over seven in ten (71%) are in favour of taxing products and services that contribute most to climate change and redistributing revenues to the poorest and most vulnerable households.

These results suggest that the narrative of a just transition centers on two priorities: using the power of the State to regulate the economy and finance investment; investing in common goods that can be used fairly by all according to their needs. A key result of the aforementioned OECD study (Dechezleprêtre, A., et al., 2022a) is indeed that the single most important determinant of support for transition policies in the availability of good quality public transports where respondents live.

Another survey[9] conducted in Belgium confirms on the one hand the holistic nature of the just transition and on the other end the key role the State should play in advancing it. Authors use a "Q methodology" to identify "typical ideal discourses" around the just transition and survey 31 organizations – associations, administrations, federations of enterprises, trade-unions, citizens' movements. Four main visions of what a "just transition" is perceived to be then emerge (Table 4.1). While Vision 2 corresponds to the narrow approach to the just transition, two much

Table 4.1 Four visions of the just transition

Vision 1: "Holistic"	Vision 2: "Workers-centered"	Vision3: "Social-ecological state"	Vision 4: "Pragmatic business-centered"
Participants associated with this vision consider the **interconnectedness of the issues related to just transition** and stress the importance of **simultaneously reducing environmental degradation and existing inequalities while guaranteeing access to fundamental rights for all**	Participants associated with this vision stress the importance of work-related issues and argue that **the just transition should first focus on the rights and conditions of workers.**	Participants associated with this vision stress the **importance of the action of the state in ensuring a just transition through taxation, investment and social security.**	Participants associated with this vision see **the just transition as a "level-playing field" for companies** and stress the importance of **guaranteeing the security of supply of energy and materials.**

Source: La Gioia, Fransolet, Hudon and Meyer (2023).

broader visions emerge with Vision 1 and Vision 3 suggesting that just transition policies should be rooted in these wide justice narratives.

RETHINKING INEQUALITY

A recent report from the European Environment Agency (EEA, 2019) highlights the close links between social and environmental issues in Europe, revealing that the distribution of air pollution, noise, extreme temperatures and their impacts on human health reflect differences in income, employment and education. These connections is anything but fortuitous: environmental degradations and ecological crises aggravate existing social inequality and trigger new ones. Hence the need to bridge dimensions of justice and forms of environmental inequality to accurately map inequality in the 21st century.

The notion of environmental inequality was born within the environmental Justice movement, which developed in the public and scientific space in the United States in the 1970s and 80s. Environmental justice can refer to different forms of inequalities: Inequality of contribution to environmental degradation; Inequality of access to amenities and environmental resources; Inequality of impact of environmental nuisances and risks; Inequality of impact of environmental policies; Inequality of participation in environmental policies.

Those different dimensions can be applied to individuals and social groups within the same generation (intra-generational justice), different generations (intergenerational justice) people belonging to different nations and states (global justice), but also justice between humans and non-humans (multi-species justice). Table 4.2 represents the combination of dimensions of justice with levels of justice that lead to mapping social-ecological inequalities.

These social-ecological inequalities call for just transition policies, i.e. new forms of public policies.

RETHINKING PUBLIC POLICY

Social-ecological policies

On the one hand, social policy have gradually developed since the end of the 19th century to address human needs and foster wellbeing. On the other end, environmental policy have gradually developed since the early 1970s to preserve ecosystems and biodiversity, i.e. the life support system of human well-being.

Social-ecological policies are policies that, today and in the long term, simultaneously reduce social inequalities and environmental degradation in synergetic policy design. One way to represent these synergies is in the form of a matrix (Figure 4.1).

Each quadrant represents a combined assessment of the social and environmental outcomes of a given situation or policy. In the upper left quadrant, energy poverty results in both monetary poverty and overconsumption of energy. Thermal insulation (home weatherization) allows a reduction in energy consumption (and therefore associated GHG emissions, triggering an environmental improvement), which results in a reduction in energy expenditure by households experiencing energy poverty (allowing for social progress). The same goes for the development of electric public transports, which reduces fuel costs for households, emissions of local (fine particles) and global (CO2) pollutants.

In the upper right quadrant, carbon taxation without social compensation is both socially regressive (it harms the poorest more due to their higher share of income spent on energy consumption) and

Table 4.2 Social-ecological inequalities

-	Intragenerational	Intergenerational	Multispecies	Global
Inequality of contribution to environmental degradation	Carbon footprint of the top 10% (50%)	Consumption of carbon budget (90% of 1.5 ° carbon budget consumed in 2023)	Ocean acidification and subsequent destruction of marine life due to human CO_2 emissions	Share of Global North in cumulative CO_2 emissions since industrial revolution (68%)
Inequality of access to amenities and environmental resources	Higher risk of water poverty with respect to income and tenure status (56,7% of at-risk-of-poverty households and 37,8% of social housing tenants affected in Belgium)	Expected future exacerbation of water scarcity associated with climate change, variable according to the extent of global warming	Impact of human appropriation of water resources on freshwater ecosystems and their biodiversity	Access to water in Nigeria (68% have access to basic water supply)
Inequality of impact of environmental nuisances and risks	Higher exposure and sensitivity to air pollution with respect to income (socio-economically disadvantaged people in poor health living in dense neighborhoods)	Higher sensitivity to air pollution linked to fossil fuels with respect to age (children and elderly)	Impact of air pollution on vegetation and biodiversity	Ecological impact of the extraction of rare Earth needed for EVs
Inequality of impact of environmental policies	Social regressivity of carbon taxation with respect to income and location (yellow vests revolt)	Low Emission Zones' impacts on job accessibility	Net zero policies impact on biodiversity	Carbon leakage

-	Intragenerational	Intergenerational	Multispecies	Global
Inequality of participation in environmental policies	Waste and toxic facilities location	Nuclear waste storage	Waste pollution in seas and oceans	Waste outsourcing (e.g. Niger delta)

Source: Fransolet and Laurent (2024).

environmentally effective (it reduces GHG emissions).[10] Introducing a modulation of taxation according to the carbon footprint and social compensation based on the level of income but also on the location (rural areas versus urban areas, suburban areas versus urban centers, etc.) maintains the environmental effectiveness of the measure (compensation should not be understood as an exemption), but mitigates its social impact and increases its political acceptability.

Finally, the lower left quadrant combines the very real need to build more affordable housing while not locking tenants or owners into the financial trap of fossil fuels whose prices are increasing and sustainably mitigating the ecological footprint of housing. In this sense, this is a just transition policy that is truly long-term.

But the logic of this synergy ban be broadened to design and implement a social-ecological matrix combining the main functions of social policy and environmental policy (Table 4.3). In this perspective, a

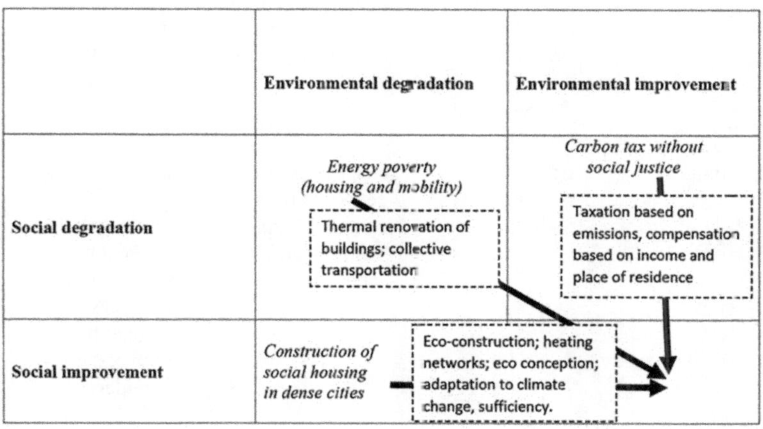

Figure 4.1 *Synergetic policy designs: Three types of just transition policies*

Table 4.3 Synergetic social-ecological policies: planetary boundaries climate biodiversity ecosystems resources

Social-ecological Policies	**Mitigation**	**Adaptation**	***Restoration and compensation***
Provision	Ensuring that low-income households have access to sufficient goods and services essential to participate in a society within planetary boundaries, including sustainable modes of housing, transport, food & water supply for all	Adequate minimum income provision to support adaptive capacity to environmental risk	Administrative assistance and cash and in-kind transfer programs for individuals, households and groups that are affected by environmental degradation and disasters
Prevention and Protection	Social insurance and social protection systems that protect against potential income losses due to shifts and shocks of the economy	Public health and disease prevention to decrease sensitivity to environmental risks; combatting social isolation, particularly among the elderly	Adapted functioning and financing of the natural disaster fund. Policies that address the insurance gap
Promotion	Education, training and reskilling programs	Deploying synergies between climate-compatible spatial planning and social cohesion	Adequate support systems for farmers enabling reorientation to agricultural practices compatible with planetary boundaries

Social-ecological Policies	**Mitigation**	**Adaptation**	***Restoration and compensation***
Transformation	Wealth and income taxation	Monitoring and accountability mechanisms of environmentally-affected social rights	Public employment *programs in the sector of ecological conservation and restoration*

Source: Laurent et al. 2024, adapted from Fransolet, A. & Vanhille, J. (eds.) (2023) Just Transition in Belgium: Concepts, Issues at Stake, and Policy Levers. Scientific report on behalf of the High Committee for a Just Transition, Brussels: November 2023.

social-ecological policy is conceived as connecting the goals and the means of social-ecological well-being. Among the goals are the key domains of essential well-being (subsistence, security, participation and stability) and their tangible dimensions (health, housing, food, social relations, political rights, etc.); among the means are public policies that must be designed so as to ensure a convergence between social and environmental domains.

Note: Well-being dimensions to be considered:

- Subsistence (food, air, water, energy);
- Security (health, housing, employment, income, civil liberties);
- Participation (social relations, political rights);
- Stability (sustainable environment, social cohesion)

As authors in Fransolet and Vanhille (2023) note, three 'routes' through to integrate social-ecological policies can be taken:

- First, many social and environmental policies already work in synergy for both social and environmental goals (e.g., energy-efficient social housing; support of social economy enterprises in the circular economy; adequate public transport; adequate unemployment benefits that protect workers against economic shocks and risks related to the transition). These are policies that can most easily be boosted, upscaled, and extended.
- Second, social concerns can explicitly be integrated into the design of environmental policies (e.g., counterbalancing gentrification

mechanisms in projects of urban greening, or progressive ecological taxation programs that avoid socially adverse consequences in their design).
- Third, environmental concerns can be integrated into the design of social policies (e.g., support for low-income households through social tariffs can, in some instances, be turned into enabling access to renewable energy infrastructures; training and reskilling programs can be oriented to support the green transition; social enterprises can be incorporated into circular economy objectives).

One specific type of social-ecological policy is sufficiency policy.

Sufficiency policies

Aristotle, arguably the Western founding thinker of economic discipline together with Xenophon, inaugurated the first age of sufficiency. He first made a clear distinction between economics (the goal of economic activity) and chrematistics (the means of acquiring resources to achieve economic goals) and, further, between good and bad chrematistics from an ethical perspective. Good chrematistics, Aristotle argues, is subordinated to economics and thus limited to acquiring resources necessary for the household to "live well" (in line with the contemporary Delphic maxim "nothing in excess" inscribed on the Temple of Apollo). The bad chrematistics on the other hand, that Aristotle labels "unnatural," escapes the law of need and morphs into a perilous appetite for unlimited resources, including monetary operations such as credit and interest (Laurent, 2023). But Aristotle also introduced the concept of "médiété" as a middle ground between contrary moral excesses (courage being defined as a middle ground between temerity and cowardice)[11]. Aristotle thus not only embeds economic activity in sufficiency reasoning but also argues for the need for sufficiency attitudes in human behaviors.

Echoing and prolonging Aristotle in his Letter to Menoeceus, Epicurus (Laurent, 2024) classifies human desires into three categories: "Natural and necessary desires" (for the well-being of the body: protecting the body against bad weather by means of fire, clothing, and shelter; for happiness; for life itself: "vital needs": hunger, thirst, rest): those are essential human needs according to Epicurus. Then come "natural and unnecessary desires" such as sexual desire and aesthetic desires; and finally, "vain/empty desires": those who go beyond the limit inherent to nature, such as the thirst for possession, power, and honors. "He who has a clear and certain understanding of these things," writes Epicurus, "will direct every preference and aversion toward securing health of body and tranquility of mind, seeing that this is the sum and end of a happy life."

The second age of sufficiency focused not on personal restraint but on collective moderation. In the early 2000s, The French NGO négaWatt (Association négaWatt, 2018) introduced this concept of sufficiency-moderation to distinguish it from the logic of energy efficiency. While energy efficiency aims at reducing the quantity of energy (and/or carbon) per unit of production, energy sufficiency ("sobriété" in French) aims at lowering the volume of energy consumed, therefore guaranteeing that moderation policies actually translate into energy savings by avoiding a "rebound effect" (or Jevons paradox) in consumption.

This contrast between sufficiency and efficiency in energy policy goes back to the emergence of the notion of optimality in neo-classical economics (at the end of the 19th century): efficiency/optimization is a relative concept which supposes that energy use is being monitored and evaluated according to an external finality, i.e., economic efficiency. Sufficiency, on the contrary is an absolute notion, where volumes and not values take center stage in the monitoring and evaluation of energy use (hence the notion of "self-sufficiency," which denotes the absence of external dependence).

négaWatt's scholars and activists insisted on the plurality of sufficiency policies:

- Structural sufficiency, which consists in reorganizing activities and space in such a way as to favor energy-efficient uses (for instance by reducing the distance between workplaces, businesses, and homes);
- Dimensional sufficiency, which aims at downscaling the size of our equipment as much as possible (for instance by reducing the size and weight of motor vehicles in urban areas often transporting a single person);
- Use sufficiency, which tends to moderate the use of energy equipment (by turning off advertising screens in subway stations or limiting speed on highways or repairing rather than replacing digital equipment);
- Collaborative sufficiency, which translates into consumption sharing (carpooling, sharing of certain domestic equipment).

Using these policies as leverages, négaWatt has for last twenty years designed energy roadmaps for France and recently European regions (CLEVER, 2023) where sufficiency, as distinguished from and combined with efficiency, is key to reduce energy demand (and that of other resources)[12].

The recently released installments of the Sixth Assessment Report (AR6) by the Intergovernmental Panel on Climate Change (IPCC) contain the first international definition of sufficiency, marking the third age of the notion. The short text, which first appeared in Chapter 9 and then Summary for Policymakers (SPM) of Working Group III Report (IPCC, 2022), found its way to the SPM of the Synthesis Report (SYR) published in March 2023 (IPCC, 2023) thanks to lead author Yamina Saheb and defines sufficiency as: "a set of policy measures and daily practices that avoid the demand for energy, materials, land, water, and other natural resources while providing well-being for all within planetary boundaries" (page 31, footnote 52). The report also provided a more precise formulation on the concept in chapter 9 (Buildings), where it is stated:

> Sufficiency addresses the issue of a fair consumption of space and resources… The remaining carbon budget, and its normative target for distributional equity, is the upper limit of sufficiency, while requirements for a decent living standard define the minimum level of sufficiency…Decent living standards are a set of essential material preconditions for human wellbeing which includes shelter, nutrition, basic amenities, health care, transportation, information, education, and public space.

This definition echoes a growing array of studies that have emphasized in recent years the potential of emissions reduction of so-called "demand-side" policies (Creutzig, Niamir, Bai et al. 2022). Hence defined, sufficiency policies appear of critical importance in mitigating climate but also biodiversity and ecosystems crises (IPCC, 2023)[13].

This very useful definition of sufficiency can be refined: on the one hand, it mixes sufficiency as a state (positive or normative) and sufficiency policies as means of achieving it; on the other, it seems to cast sufficiency policies as demand policies only (as opposed to supply). It is thus useful to specify that, on the one hand, sufficiency as a state positively designates a situation or space[14] in which limited resources are used to satisfy reasoned needs which can result in a state defined normatively as a universal decent living standard compatible with planetary boundaries. On the other end, sufficiency policies can be defined as measures aimed at ensuring this compatibility (possibly through the use of consumption and production "corridors")[15].

Sufficiency, as it is defined above, relies on three conditions:

- The existence of a sufficient level of human well-being compatible with the Biosphere's viability; this means that the planet should be part of the design;
- This sufficient level of human well-being is one that is not excessive nor insufficient (the state of sufficiency possibly taking the form of a space or "sufficiency corridor"); this means that excess and insufficiency should be part of the design;
- Sufficiency policies allow to move into the sufficiency space/corridor and to stay there.

In geography, the terrestrial equator is an imaginary line drawn around our planet, halfway to the poles, marking the separation between the northern hemisphere and the southern hemisphere with a latitude of 0°. The "social equator" (Figure 4.2) is also an imaginary line representing the level of human well-being compatible with the viability of the Biosphere, bringing down excessive modes of consumption and production and lifting up insufficient well-being conditions globally[16].

On the right end side of the figure, the state of sufficiency (the social equator), the sufficiency corridor and its boundaries are represented. Those boundaries correspond to the "safe and just Earth system boundaries" recently highlighted in the planetary boundaries literature (Rockström, Gupta, Qin et al., 2023)[17]. On the left end side of the figure, excessive and insufficient well-being conditions are ordered according to the global distribution of income and wealth (Chancel et al. 2022).

At the center of the figure, sufficiency policies allow to reach the sufficiency corridor (for instance via social-ecological taxation and transfer, Laurent 2023) but also to stay within its limits (focusing on the interlinkages between cooperation, health and justice, see the "social-ecological feedback loop" presented in Laurent, 2023).

The Social-ecological state

Our era of social inequality and ecological shocks calls for a deep transformation of our welfare state into a social-ecological state, able to provide social-ecological protection of human well-being in the face of

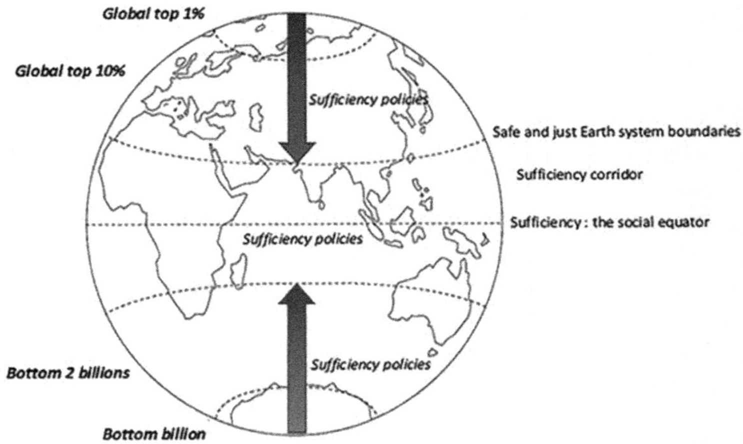

Note: The climate crisis provides tentative empirical estimates of this visualization. Ending extreme poverty (of some 700 million people) has a negligible impact on global emissions (Wollburg, Hallegatte, & Mahler, 2023) while emissions from the top 1% and top 10% are considerable (representing respectively 17% and 48% of total emissions, see Chancel, 2022). In a country like France, the bottom 50% of the population is already at the level of emissions compatible with the Paris Treaty goals (Chancel, 2022), in other words close to the safe and just earth system boundary regarding climate.
Source: own elaboration.

Figure 4.2 The social equator

climate change, the destruction of biodiversity and the degradation of ecosystems visible and tangible everywhere on the planet. Yet, as the IPCC AR6 report (IPCC, 2023) makes clear, this social-ecological state should not come at the cost of further unsustainable economic growth that would further increase social risk. We thus need to provide and protect without growing, we need to invent welfare beyond growth.

To understand the framework of the social-ecological state, a good point of departure is the new trilemma (or 'impossible trinity') that has materialised at the beginning of the twenty-first century, with the welfare state, economic growth and ecological transition as vertices (Figure 4.3).

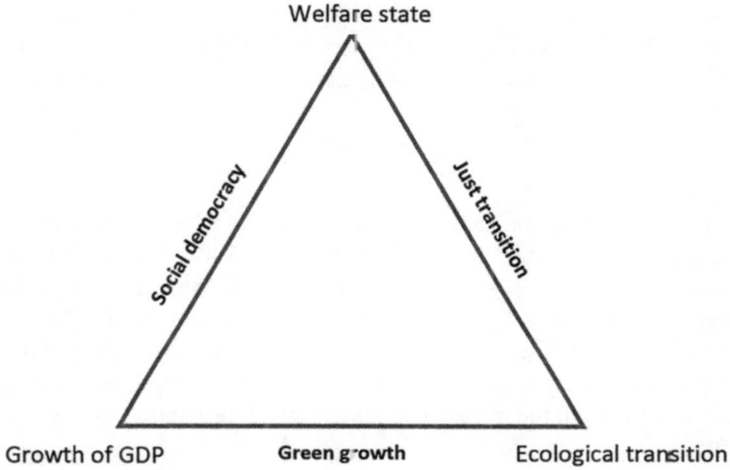

Note: pick two vertices, only two.
Source: Author

Figure 4.3 *The welfare-growth-transition trilemma*

BOX 4.1 READING: ONE PAST, TWO FUTURES

'**Social democracy**' denotes the social-economic alliance characteristic of the post-war decades in Western European countries, where social policy and economic growth went hand in hand without consideration for environmental degradation (at least until the early 1970s): economic growth stabilises the welfare state but without regard for the biosphere's destabilisation.

'**Green growth**' uses ecological transition as a means to increase GDP growth, thought to be a source of trickle-down prosperity. In this scenario, ecosystems continue to be heavily damaged at least in the medium term and this degradation gradually renders welfare states financially unsustainable because of the resulting human health degradation: the welfare state is destabilised and eventually derailed by the pursuit of growth.

'**Just transition**' puts the mutualisation and equalisation power of the welfare state at the service of ecological transition, building a social-ecological transition that combines sustainability and justice, abandons GDP growth as a collective horizon and focuses on policies that simultaneously reduce natural resource consumption and social inequality.

Social stability can be said to be the overall goal of the welfare state and it largely explains why it was founded in 1880s' unified Germany. The aim of political stabilization through social stabilization is indeed transparent in Kaiser Wilhelm Royal Proclamation on Social Policy of November 17, 1881 which states: "curing social defects will have to be pursued not only through the repression of Social Democratic excesses but also through the consistent and positive promotion of workers' welfare".

This pursuit of social stability was even clearer when European nations sought to grow their welfare states after World War 2 and use it as a tool to tame capitalist systems and their inherent volatility that destabilized European societies in the 1930s. In the post war decades, it was believed that economic growth was the vector of social stability through its ability to fund the welfare state. The political compromises between the interests of employees and capitalists were based on the assumption that high employment level and progressive taxation would reduce economic inequality and support public services while capital remained intact, and capitalist economic growth was encouraged[18].

Yet, it is more and more obvious that this stability has morphed into a growth dependency that itself is resulting in unsustainability. To put it simply, what is at stake in the early 21st century is to build welfare states that support and enable well-being within planetary boundaries[19], and currently economic growth appears as a force of destabilization in this respect.

Welfare states vary in terms of goals, governance, and financing but, as a branch of public finance, they all share three core functions: allocation, redistribution and stabilization[20].

Allocation refers to the provision of public goods (or the delineation of the border between public goods and private goods by the state). With this function, welfare states are able to correct market misallocation of resources (e.g. insufficient vaccination based on private cost rather than social cost considerations leading to "market failure" in this case suboptimal vaccination rates among the population).

Economic growth is detrimental to the allocation function in two ways. First, through commodification, it increases the cost of social protection provision. While public services are being privatized in the name of economic growth, inefficiency increases, as do costs of all kinds. There is no better example of this allocation destabilization than the US healthcare system[21].

In addition to this direct destabilization, an indirect one has emerged in the form of increased costs due to growing social risks induced by ecological crises. One example is the growing cost of climate change and the impossibility of public insurance to cover the damage of so-called natural disasters[22].

Distribution refers to the collection and redistribution of taxes and social contributions to finance public services and social benefits reflecting the collective preferences of citizens in matters of justice.

Here also, the priority given to economic growth has a direct and indirect effect on the welfare state's ability to perform distribution.

First, economic growth policies have been focused on lowering taxes, especially on the most mobile bases such as high-income individuals, corporations and capital owners. As a result, the welfare state has been deprived of vital resources (in the EU, social and tax competition has resulted in lowering corporate tax rates lower than the global average) and the distribution function has been weakened on the taxation side.

But ecological crises additionally and directly weaken this function by increasing the need for revenues, given the increased social vulnerability (understood as a product of exposure and sensitivity) of certain groups (such as the elderly in the face of more frequent and intense heatwaves) or localities (such as coastal regions).

Finally, according to Musgrave (1959), the welfare state performs a *stabilization* function: it uses public finance as an instrument to buffer economic shocks using automatic stabilizers such as unemployment benefits and income taxation. From this stabilization perspective, "growing" the economy through financialization means increasing the intensity and frequency of financial crises. Such has been the case in the 1990s and of course with the "great recession" of 2008–2009, which led to massive social spending, for instance through unemployment benefits and a substantial destabilization of pensions systems (for instance in France) through the reduction of employment rates, and at least a decade of financial setback for welfare states (as in the case of the French pension system, which was financially sound in 2008).

Because ecological crises are risks which call for new forms of collective protection, the social-ecological State must be constituted at the early 21st century to protect human well-being by pooling ecological risk, as the social state has done successfully for almost a century and a half with all the major social risks linked to work: unemployment, old age, illness, disability, etc. The social-ecological state can thus become the key institution of the just transition and its rationale is no different than that of social protection: to sustain human well-being in the face of damaging shocks by pooling risk and mitigating inequality.

A brief look at the last few years in the world is enough to see that contemporary ecological crises (first and foremost climate change) constitute powerful vectors of social risks: giant fires, floods, storms, tornadoes and pandemics have disrupted the lives of billion people on the planet including in affluent regions like the European Union.

While between 1980 and 1999, the overall cost of storms, floods, heatwaves, cold waves, droughts and forest fires totalled 175 billion euros in the EU, they amounted to 245 billion euros between 2000 and 2019, close to 1,5 more. These costs are going to increase much further in coming years[23]. Of these losses today, private insurance covers 25% on average in EU countries (60% at best), largely for wealthy households. Ecological crises are social risk threatening the lives and livelihoods of Europeans, especially the most vulnerable ones: close to 100 000 Europeans have died because of these increasingly violent ecological shocks in the last four decades, many more have been driven to poverty or precariousness by losing their homes, equipment and social networks. We know for sure that these human losses are going to skyrocket if we don't build adequate collective social-ecological protections.

By the same token, a recent briefing[24] by the EEA shows that between 1980 and 2020, total economic losses from weather- and climate-related events amounted to EUR 450–520 billion euros in the 32 EEA member countries (EEA-32) and 145 billion euros in the last decade alone with the highest total loss recorded in 2017 (€27.9 billion). With temperatures in Europe increasing at more than twice the global average over the past 30 years (the highest of any continent in the world), studies converge toward a significant economic and human potential toll in coming decades for EU member states. We have indeed entered a world where social-ecological risks are skyrocketing.

Social protection consists, since its invention in Bismarck's Germany in 1883, almost a century and a half ago, of pooling social risks to reduce social injustices and the economic inefficiencies they cause due to a lack of insurance. Social risks are now driven in large part by ecological crises, hence the need to move from social protection to social-ecological protection.

The security function at the foundation of a Welfare state which intends to measure, supervise and plan society, is based on the distinction established in 1921 by British economist Frank Knight between risk and uncertainty: risk is measurable uncertainty while uncertainty cannot be apprehended via human calculation.

If a risk is an uncertain, probable event, a social risk is an uncertain, probable event of a collective nature, either in terms of responsibility or in terms of impact. It can become insurable (covered and compensated) by an insurance mechanism that is itself collective if we manage to precisely determine both the probability (occurrence) and the associated monetary and non-monetary losses (intensity of the impact). A social-ecological risk is thus an uncertain probabilistic event of a collective nature linked to the occurrence of an ecological shock defined as a cyclical or structural alteration of the environmental conditions of existence affecting human well-being (pollution, climate shock, pandemic shock, etc.).

If social life under ecological crises became totally uncertain, then it would be futile to want to protect human well-being by means of insurance and the welfare state would not be able to protect human well-being. But if social-ecological shocks become risks, then their apparent inevitability can be normalized, standardized and shared. Public action then evolves from unpredictable individual risks to a manageable social risk, calculated and mutualized. Social-ecological protection aims precisely at covering and pooling social-ecological risks.

On top of exposure to social-ecological risk, exposure to air pollution, fuel poverty (housing and mobility), poor nutritional quality of food, noise, etc. are environmental degradations that first affects the most fragile and vulnerable. If ecological shocks hit populations, environmental degradation undermines their resistance and their ability to come back to life.

This is why it is vital to combine a real effort to invest in prevention with an effort to anticipate ecological shocks, in other words to build a "social-ecological prevention" pillar beside the "social-ecological protection" pillar to sustain the social-ecological state.

NOTES

1. Authors of Fondation de l'écologie politique (Fondation de l'écologie politique, 2023) show that 88% of yellow vests consider climate change to be real (90% in France), 75% that it is mainly due to human activities (73% in France) and 74% that mitigating climate change should be a political priority (73% in France).
2. Many options of just transition policy exist. While keeping 55 euros per ton of carbon in 2021 as an environmental objective and redistributing 25% of revenues to households using already existing mechanisms, a majority of households (more than 50% of households in the first 6 deciles of standard of living)14 gain from carbon taxation (receiving more in social transfers than what they pay in carbon taxation). The 75% of the remaining revenue can be allocated to the fight fuel poverty but also to provide financial help to shift to low-carbon equipment, reducing social inequality further (Laurent and Berry, 2019).
3. See Andersson and Atkinson (2020), Bourgeois et al. (2019) or Douenne (2018).
4. Dechezleprêtre, A., et al. (2022a).
5. Authors note that "Subsidies for low-carbon technologies and public investments in green technologies and infrastructures (financed by public debt) receive more than 55% support in high-income countries and more than 65% support in middle-income countries. There is equally high support for the mandatory and subsidized insulation of residential buildings across countries."
6. European Commission, 2023b.
7. Ipsos/BNP Paribas (2023).
8. "Grant aid to individuals to make housing more energy efficient, particularly for the most vulnerable households"; "Increase the country's investment in public transport infrastructure"; "Encourage private companies to reduce their emissions more quickly"; "Tax the products and services that contribute the most to climate change and redistribute the revenue to the poorest households"; "Allocate an energy quota to each citizen".
9. La Gioia, Fransolet, Hudon and Meyer (2023).
10. Cf. supra the analysis of the « yellow vests » crisis in France.
11. Morel, 2020.
12. Based on energy sufficiency, energy efficiency, and renewable sources energy transition scenarios can reach 100% renewables by 2050.
13. The potential of demand-side mitigation options by 2050 ranges from 29% of reduction in emissions for industry up to 67% for land transport and 73% for electricity.

14. Gough (2023) defines sufficiency as "the space above the floor of necessity but below the ceiling of excess".
15. See respectively Di Giulio and Fuchs, 2014 and Bärnthaler and Gough, 2023.
16. "The distance to the equator" is a metric commonly used in inequality economics literature to account for development inequality, see Theil and Fink, 1983.
17. When assessing where humans stand with respect to planetary boundaries regarding climate, the biosphere, fresh water, nutrients and air pollution at global and subglobal scales, the authors use not just "safe" quantitative thresholds for maintaining Earth system resilience but also three justice criteria (Interspecies justice , Intergenerational justice and Intragenerational justice). As a result, some boundaries become more stringent: for climate, while the "safe" limit stands close to 1,5°C, the safe and just limit is set at 1°C, a threshold that human societies have already exceeded.
18. Hirvilammi 2020
19. According to the latest estimates, humanity is outside the safe operating space of six planetary boundaries including the loss of biosphere integrity, climate change, land system change, altered nitrogen and phosphorous flows, and the planetary boundary for novel entities (Persson et al. 2022). The impacts of transgressing the planetary boundaries may not be instant but the uncertainty will rise: the farther the boundary is transgressed, the higher will be the risks of destabilized ecosystem processes. Crossing the boundaries gives societies fewer opportunities to prepare for system changes. (Steffen et al. 2015)
20. Musgrave 1959
21. See Laurent, 2023
22. According to reinsurer Swiss Re, so-called "natural" disasters resulted in more than $175 billion in losses in 2020. Three facts are worth noting in this regard. First, the number of events considered catastrophic has risen sharply over the past forty years, from 249 to 820. Over this period there was a 151% increase in direct economic losses due to climate-related disasters, which represent 77% of total losses (https://www.swissre.com/institute/research/sigma-research.html). Globally, less than half of these losses – around USD 76 billion – have been insured (in developping countries, this share is close to 10% on average). According to Munich Re, worldwide, out of 5.2 trillion dollars of losses incurred since 1980 because of so-called "natural disasters", 3,745 are counted as uninsured and 1,491 as insured (about three quarters against one quarter).
23. According to EEA data https://www.eea.europa.eu/data-and-maps/daviz/impacts-of-extreme-weather-and-2#tab-chart_1
24. EEA (2021).

5. Rethinking the economy and democracy

RETHINKING THE ECONOMY

Economics, in its current forms, both as an intellectual discipline (neoclassical economics mixed with occasional Keynesianism) and as a system of organizing society (digital neoliberal capitalism), poses a vital risk to humanity; it must reform itself in depth by taking note of the new biophysical situation that it itself has generated and by refocusing on the imperative of social justice, which has long been its reason for being. The economy in the 21st century must therefore be an embedded economy, bounded by upstream biophysics, with, as a frontier discipline, ecological economics (which studies material flows, waste, energy, biodiversity, ecosystems, etc.), and bounded downstream by social justice, with, as a boundary discipline, political economy (which highlights social inequalities and measures the quality of political institutions). And it is an economy of essential well-being, which articulates universal human needs with planetary ecological constraints by projecting them over time. This well-being economy, compatible with just transitions, is fundamentally post-growth.

The post-growth agenda is decades, if not centuries old and can be said to have preceded the invention of modern economic growth measurement by Simon Kuznets in 1934[1]. Currently, the expression "post-growth" is used as an umbrella term gathering different alternatives to standard growth-focused economic visions (Büchs and Koch, 2017) and indicators (Laurent, 2018). In this respect, it is important to note from the onset that "Beyond GDP" and "post-growth" agendas, while overlapping, are not synonymous. Post-growth, understood as an intellectual movement, can be broadly defined as "an era in which the societal project is redefined beyond the pursuit of growth"[2]. But it was preceded by the "Beyond GDP" agenda, whose tentative starting point in the contemporary period is November 2007, when the European Union (EU) co-organized the first institutional international conference on the matter[3].

At this event (attended by around 600 participants), the goal was to map the field of alternative indicators to Gross Domestic Product (GDP) and showcase attempts to complement EU governance metrics with those indicators, but it was not to offer alternative visions stemming from consolidated academic communities. Then EU Commission President Barroso outlined his expectations for the outcome of the conference in clear terms: "adapt GDP, or complement it with indicators that are better suited to our needs today, and the challenges we face today." In his closing argument, Stavros Dimas, then Commissioner for Environment and initiator of the conference, remarked that "the main achievement of this conference has been to clearly demonstrate the political consensus on the need to go beyond GDP."

The communication "GDP and Beyond: Measuring Progress in a Changing World,"[4] released in 2009 by the European Commission (EC, 2009), was intended as a follow-up to the 2007 Conference. It described ways to improve indicators in order to better reflect the societal concerns of Europeans, but it is fair to say that very little has happened since then in EU policymaking. In short, the 2007 conference was about adapting indicators to new economic realities but not about shifting paradigms, and it fell short of its limited objectives.

About fifteen years later, the landscape looks quite different academically, and the policy space created within the EU appears much larger, as reflected by the May 2023 Conference organized by the European Parliament and dozens of NGOs and attended by thousands of participants, aptly titled "Beyond Growth-Pathways towards Sustainable Prosperity in the EU." The focus was explicitly put on superseding growth as a social paradigm rather than just perfecting or completing GDP as an indicator and on policy reforms rather than technical adjustments[5].

This event showcased post-growth scholar communities and their policy allies (trade unions, activists, politicians, NGOs) coming together at the call of the key democratic EU institution, the European Parliament. It coincided with an unprecedented effort by the EU to support post-growth studies with half a dozen new projects funded by ERC and EU Horizon programs in 2023 alone. It was the moment when three major consolidated post-growth streams emerged together on the European and international scene – degrowth, Doughnut economy, and Wellbeing economy – displaying their academic credentials (visible publications and well-funded research projects) and policymaking achievements (tangible influence on international and national debates and policies).

The ill-being economy: the pathologies of growth

In the course of the 20th century, human well-being has seen an unprecedented expansion mostly driven by improvements in health (between 1870 and 2007, human well-being has increased by a factor of 6, health improvement accounting for 47% of the increase while improvements in education account for 38% and the rise of income per capita for 15%, Figure 5.1).

Medical and technical innovations, which made it possible to decipher, contain, and eventually repel infectious diseases in the first half of the 20th century, improving the health of youth and then allowing for greater longevity of the elderly in the second half of the 20th century, obviously played a key role in this progress. But so did the continuous democratization of the quality of life acquired through the extension and erection of labor laws and social protections, the expansion of public

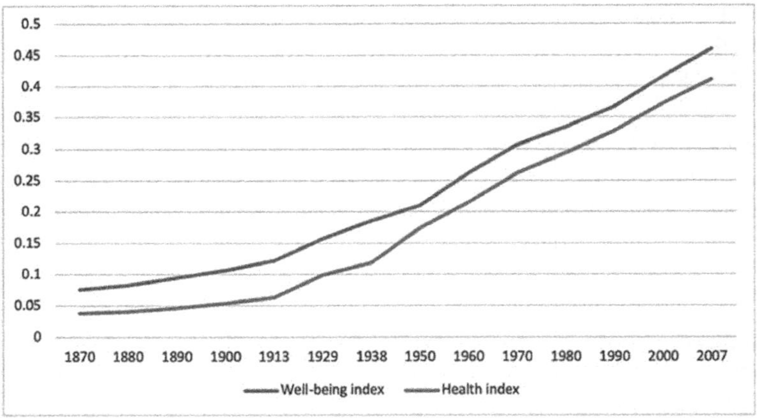

Note: Human well-being is measured by the Historical Human Development Index (HHDI), a historical variant of the UN HDI, which averages indices of life expectancy at birth, education, and income levels. Health is measured by an index of life expectancy at birth.
Source: Prados de la Escosura (2015).

Figure 5.1 *An unprecedented human well-being progress driven by health, 1870–2007*

education and public health, and the generalization of better hygiene and healthier diets.

Human health, the core of human well-being, is indeed determined by social conditions: social dynamics are the central determinants of salutogenesis (what enables health)[6] as well as pathogenesis (what drives disease)[7] of human populations. Health studies have made remarkable progress in the last 25 years in precisely identifying the social and ecological determinants of human health. At least three major insights have been widely documented:

- The importance of economic and social conditions (commercial determinants and health inequities) for biological and mental health;
- The importance of good social relations for mental health, happiness, and life expectancy;
- The importance of viable environmental conditions and the thriving health of non-humans (ecosystems, plants, and animals) for maintaining human health.

Let's briefly review in turn the evidence at hand on those three insights. There is first an inextricable link between health and social justice. Numerous studies, initiated in the United Kingdom by Richard Wilkinson, Kate Pickett, and Michael Marmot, demonstrate the negative impact of social inequalities on physical and mental health (Wilkinson and Pickett, 2006; Marmot, 2010 and 2018). The recent update of the Marmot review (Marmot et al., 2020) shows for instance, how the contemporary decline in life expectancy in the most deprived communities of the UK after decades of continuous progress is related to austerity imposed on public services and the disintegration social crisis that resulted. The late Paul Farmer insisted on the role of inequalities in the developing world as a "plague" just as damaging to human health as the worst pathogens (Farmer, 1999).

Social and economic conditions, it is now understood, and their effects on people's lives determine their risk of illness, the measures taken to prevent them from getting sick, or to treat pathologies when they occur[8]. These social determinants of health (the circumstances in which people are born, grow, live, work, and age and the healthcare systems to which people have access throughout their life cycle) induce health inequalities understood as systematic relationships between health and social criteria (gender, nationality, ethnicity, family composition, income and assets, level of education, etc.). In all countries, health strongly depends on these social determinants, which are in turn shaped by a broader set of institutional forces: the economic system, social policies, and political dynamics. Within those institutional forces, new studies highlight the role of "commercial determinants" of health (Kickbusch, Allen, and Franz, 2016 and Petticrew, Glover, Volmink et al., 2023)[9].

The second insight concerns the relationship between health and social relations. The Harvard Study of Adult Development (HSAD)[10], unique in its length and depth, yields a clear-cut result: good social relationships best explain mental and biological health outcomes over time (i.e., the longevity and declared felicity of participants). Conversely, studies have revealed the considerable health penalties associated with loneliness and social isolation (Holt-Lunstad and Perissinotto, 2023).

Finally, it appears that no human health can be sustained without the underlying health of ecosystems and biodiversity that underpin it. Hence the concept of "planetary health," defined as "the health of human civilization and the state of the natural systems on which it depends" (Horton et al. 2015). Hence, also, the so-called "One Health" approach insisting on the complementarity and interdependence of human health, animal health, plant health, and environmental health:

> One Health is an integrated, unifying approach that aims to sustainably balance and optimize the health of people, animals and ecosystems.
>
> It recognizes the health of humans, domestic and wild animals, plants, and the wider environment (including ecosystems) are closely linked and inter-dependent.
>
> The approach mobilizes multiple sectors, disciplines and communities at varying levels of society to work together to foster well-being and tackle threats to health and ecosystems, while addressing the collective need for clean water, energy and air, safe and nutritious food, taking action on climate change, and contributing to sustainable development.[11]

In the face of these three insights, contemporary economic systems (which have been founded on the pursuit of economic growth since the post-war period)[12] appear triply irrational: they foster social inequalities[13] and harmful commercial practices[14] instead of mitigating them, they foster social isolation[15] instead of good social relations, they destroy the living world instead of preserving it.[16] Current production and consumption structures, directly and indirectly, in the short and long run, jeopardize the social and ecological foundations of human health as highlighted by recent advances in health studies.

In contrast with this evidence, conventional economics has long argued that economic growth would lead to better health ("wealth is health"[17]) based on a cursory and partial reading of a classic paper by Preston (1975)[18]. Yet, recent and comprehensive empirical investigations point to a "weak and statistically insignificant" association between GDP growth and human health (UNDP, 2010; Easterly 1999) and even highlight "diminishing returns" of economic growth (Paulsson, Koch and Fritz, 2024). Unsurprisingly, health policies understood in a broad sense (access to care, social protection labor law, etc.) best explain health outcomes (Deaton, 2013). What is more, medical scholars and professional associations have recently advocated moving away from GDP as a compass, making the case for the health cost associated with "uneconomic growth" (Hensher et al. 2020) and arguing that "the current policy focus on economic growth is damaging population health" (Modi, 2022). The well-being economy offers a vision and practical policies out of the pathologies of economic growth.

Defining the Well-being economy

The well-being economy is the most recent stream of post-growth studies to have emerged in the aftermath of the 2008–2009 "great recession" (Fioramonti et al., 2022). Scholars involved in the "Well-being Economy Alliance," created in 2018, have attempted to characterize its specificities in the flourishing field of beyond growth or post-growth studies and have defined the well-being economy as "an economy that pursues human and ecological wellbeing […] well suited to travel across cultures and penetrate policy processes because it links with values and concepts that are shared by a number of societies," contrasting it with degrowth (Fioramonti et al., 2022). While the universal nature of human health is not considered by those scholars to be the core identity of the well-being economy, it should, as evidenced by the recent "Well-being economy initiative" of the World Health Organization (2023), the "Health in the Well-Being Economy" Regional Forum (held in Copenhagen on 1–2 March 2023), and the first "Well-being Economy Forum" (held in Reykjavik on June 14–15 of 2023).

Historically, well-being has been connected to health as early as the appearance of the term "wellness" (meaning the "state of being well or in good health") in the English language in the mid-17th century (Oxford English Dictionary, 2016). Well-being, built from Latin words "bene" and "stare" which together mean "being well", is currently defined as "the state of being comfortable, healthy, or happy", a definition insisting on the multi-dimensionality of human health (at least psychological and physiological). Indeed, well-being refers to a self-reflection on health, a personal and subjective judgment on one's objective health, echoing modern exploration of the importance of mental health for biological health. What is more, well-being can be applied to different scales (individual, social, and even national), revealing its social underpinning. This underpinning is apparent in the 19th century notion of "welfare" introduced in Kaiser Wilhelm I's Royal Proclamation on Social Policy of 17 November 1881 (recognizing "workers' welfare" and acknowledging "a legitimate claim to a greater degree of state welfare"). Welfare, understood as social well-being, is obviously the cornerstone of social policy expansion in the 19th and 20th centuries (the "welfare state"). Recent work has put forth the notion of "social-ecological well-being" (Laurent, 2023 and Nayak and Pradhan, 2023) as an attempt to conceive human well-being as embedded in social institutions and biophysical realities.

Well-being can thus be defined as *a holistic approach to human health*, physical and psychological, individual and social, human and ecological (Laurent, 2023), a definition consistent with the 1948 World Health Organization Constitution, which states: "Health is a state of complete physical, mental, and social well-being and not merely the absence of disease or infirmity."

From these developments, the well-being economy is an *a post-growth economy that generates sufficient human well-being,* i.e. an economy centered on reasoned needs (reasoned in the sense of resulting from collective discussion on social-ecological justice principles) met by limited resources within planetary boundaries (and not on infinite growth that would trickle down on human needs nor on utility preferences satisfaction as in the neo-classical economics framework). Two core domains of well-being appear critical in this perspective: health in its three dimensions (individual, collective, and ecological) and cooperation in its three dimensions (social relations, social justice, and democracy).

The well-being economy should not be interpreted as a watered-down version of post-growth compatible with GDP expansion where health itself becomes the source of new economic growth. Anchored on a non-instrumental holistic approach to human health, the well-being economy actually implies a paradigm shift away from standard economics, which has largely colonized health studies. Following in the footsteps of Gary Becker, Grossman (1972) proposed more than fifty years ago to consider health as a form of human capital, described as a stock of assets depreciating with aging, in which individuals can choose to invest to obtain the return they desire. This conceptual imperialism has been preceded ever since the post-war period by the development of metrics aimed at monetizing human health[19].

The economic instrumentation of health is in full display in the philosophy and recommendations of the High-Level Commission on Health Employment and Economic Growth appointed in March 2016 by then UN Secretary Ban Ki-moon, which argues that "economic growth and development depend on a healthy population" and advocates for "targeted investment in health systems" in order to "promote economic growth" (High-Level Commission on Health Employment and Economic Growth, 2016). Contrary to this instrumental approach, the WHO Council on the Economics of Health for All's recent report affirms that: "A healthy population is not just human and social capital, or a by-product of economic growth. Health is a fundamental human right. Alongside a healthy and sustainable environment, human health and wellbeing must be the ultimate goal of economic activity."[20]

RETHINKING DEMOCRACY

Anti-environmental populism is gaining momentum in the EU and the US. This is particularly true, but not exclusively, on the right-end of the political spectrum. Anti-environmental populism relies on two core arguments. The first consists of simply denying the environmental emergency and replacing it with concerns about national identity. The second consists of weaponizing social emergency against environmental emergency. The false narrative, according to which environmental protection can be separated from social protection and is always counter to social and economic goals, is feeding this dogmatic movement. While these ideological positions are presented in the public debate as popular demands, they actually stand in flagrant contradiction with European values and European's aspirations[21].

In public opinion surveys, EU citizens express an unmistakable twin social and environmental priority. The Autumn 2023 delivery of the Eurobarometer showed, for instance that six months before the European elections, the three policy demands of EU citizens were, ranked by importance: 1) the fight against poverty and social exclusion; 2) public health; and 3) climate crisis mitigation.

More structurally, the Eurobarometer points to rare good news: a large majority of Europeans support a fair green transition. Yet, Eurobarometer data also show that EU citizens feel this green transition is and might be socially unfair in the future[22]. This reflects the fact that tens of millions are suffering today in the EU from the high cost of living and poor environmental conditions.

What this means is that the environmental emergency is very real in the eyes of EU citizens who call for a better articulation between social and environmental issues. The Eurobarometer provides clear evidence that citizens rather consider environmental and social issues as joint priorities instead of opposed ones. Hence the need to design and implement just transition policies democratically, by ensuring citizen understanding, support, and participation.

Just transitions are a good example of what Elinor Ostrom (2010) has called "polycentric transitions": each level of government can seize this opportunity to reform its policies without waiting for the impetus to come from above, and meaningful initiatives can come from any level of government. These initiatives are based on the fact that just transitions aim at precise goals (i.e., reducing greenhouse gas emissions while also reducing income inequality), but also a method to achieve these goals so that new political methods are required to articulate environmental and social issues.

Open democracy

In the words of political scientist Hélène Landemore (Landemore, 2020), "Open Democracy describes a new model of democracy that opens up power to ordinary citizens" and could "strengthen inclusiveness, responsiveness, and accountability in modern societies."

"Citizens' conferences" are an example of open democracy: they often include a panel of citizens, experts, and decision-makers discussing the respective importance of different dimensions of well-being and agreeing on policies to implement the priorities they have commonly set.

This is precisely the purpose of Scotland's Just Transition Commission, which is based on the principle that "a just transition is both the outcome – a fairer, greener future for all – and the process that must be undertaken in partnership with those impacted by the transition to net zero. It supports a net-zero and climate resilient economy in a way that delivers fairness and tackles inequality and injustice."

To support the delivery of this ambition, the Scottish Government has committed to leading the production of key just transition plans, in a way that is co-designed and co-delivered by communities, businesses, unions, workers, and all of society. The key roles of the Just Transition Commission will be to support the production and monitoring of such plans, providing expert advice on their development.

Specifically, the Commission is tasked with[23]:

- providing scrutiny and advice on the ongoing development of Scottish Government-led just transition plans, including the application of the Just Transition Planning Framework
- advising on the most suitable approaches to monitoring and evaluation
- undertaking meaningful engagement with those most likely to be impacted by the transition, hearing from a broad range of representative voices, and advising on how to ensure these can shape and contribute to just transition planning work in Scotland
- engaging and collaborating with other sources of expertise, including relevant Scottish Government advisory bodies and relevant programs of work (including, but not limited to, the Committee on Climate Change, the Poverty and Inequality Commission, the Fair Work Convention, the Council of Economic Advisors, and the development of the National Strategy for Economic Transformation)
- publishing an annual report to reflect on Scotland's progress

The embedment of such initiatives in existing representative democracy institutions is key to their success. In the case of Scotland's Just Transition Commission, this embedment takes two forms[24]:

- At the start of each work year, the Minister for Just Transition, Employability, and Fair Work will write to the Commission advising them of planned government work that can help inform the development of the Commission's own work plan. Scottish Ministers may also make ad-hoc requests for advice in support of just transition planning. The independent commission will be responsible for developing its own work plan with support from the Just Transition Commission Secretariat.
- In the process of carrying out its functions, the Commission will be expected to engage widely with those likely to be affected by the transition to net-zero, particularly with the business sector, workers, trade unions, community organizations, and young people. It will also be expected to take into account wider equalities including all protected characteristics. There will be a budget to support additional

information and evidence gathering. This will be for the purpose of identifying gaps and helping shape research questions, rather than carrying out major primary research per se.

When citizens' commissions are not embedded in existing institutions in a clear way, their contribution is minimized, regardless of the quality of deliberations between citizens, a peril clearly illustrated by the French "Convention Citoyenne pour le Climat." In the wake of the "Yellow Vests" crisis and the "Great National Debate" decided and organized by the government, a collective called the "Citizen Vests" (led by the director and poet Cyril Dion and the actress Marion Cotillard) offered to President Emmanuel Macron in January 2019 to organize a "citizen assembly" to discuss, in particular the social issues raised by the ecological transition. The proposal was accepted in the spring, and 150 representative citizens (according to gender, age, level of diploma, socio-professional category, type of territory, and geographical area) (Fabre et al., 2021) were collectively entrusted with the following mandate: "Define structuring measures to achieve, in a spirit of social justice, a reduction in GHG emissions by at least 40% by 2030 compared to 1990." The "Convention Citoyenne pour le Climat" (or CCC), as it came to be known, is thus probably the most specifically purposed citizens' assembly when it comes to just transition.

Monitored in real-time by a battery of observers and researchers, the convention members worked for nine months and unanimously approved, on June 21 149 measures proposed around four main themes: "Consumption" (14 measures), "Mobility" (43), "Housing" (21), and "Food" (43), the remaining 28 measures being scattered across a variety of areas. Only one measure, related to the reduction of working hours, was proposed for voting but eventually rejected. The quality of the consensus was thus nearing perfection, and the quality of the work carried out was widely praised by both experts and environmental organizations and associations (Giraudet et al., 2020).

In his speech of April 25, 2019, the French President of the Republic Emmanuel Macron committed to submitting directly and in their integrity ("without filter") the measures proposed via referendum, parliamentary vote, or direct regulatory application. This non-binding commitment would ultimately result in a partial and watered-down adoption of a fraction of the 149 proposals in the "Climate and Resilience" law adopted on August 22, 2021 (according to convergent counts, around 90% of the

Convention's proposals have not been implemented, with the members of the Convention giving a score of 3.3/10 to the use of their work by the executive and legislative powers).

In addition to the quality of the work accomplished in a short period of time by a citizens' assembly, the orientation of the measures recommended by the Convention proves rich in lessons for just transition policies. The members of the Convention, in fact considered that social justice would be served more by regulation and standards than by taxation (of the 149 measures ultimately adopted, 76 were of a regulatory nature and only 11 of a fiscal nature), an outcome that echoes insights from studies reviewed in the "reinventing justice narratives" section. Interestingly enough, Lage et al. (2023) show that European Citizen Assemblies are indeed recommending far more measures that revolve around sufficiency than their governments in the National Energy and Climate Plans (NECP).

Multi-level democracy: the case of the EU

Europe is the continent where, at the end of the 19th century, well-being was invented as a public policy objective with the first laws giving birth to the welfare state (starting in Germany in the 1880s). But the European Union has also defined itself since its origin (at the beginning of the 1990s) as a normative, post-materialist power, which intends to go beyond the traditional criteria and attributes of power and sovereignty and work to mitigate ecological crises. The European model or identity, however complex and elusive, has strong connections with the just transition approach, and the new European strategy unveiled in December 2019, the European Green Deal, seems to embrace a form of social-ecological transition, affirming at once its will to become "the first climate-neutral continent" in a transition that "leaves no one behind" (European Commission 2019). Yet, the European Commission Communication (European Commission 2019) defined from the onset the European Green Deal as a "new growth strategy" and mobilized concepts and instruments which mainly aim at economic efficiency and marginally social justice (tellingly, the word "inequality" is absent from the text).

The European Green Deal therefore aspires to be a just transition strategy but is closer in reality to the notion of "green growth," which was defined by the OECD as follows: "Green growth consists of promoting economic growth and development while ensuring that natural assets continue to provide the resources and environmental services on which our well-being depends. To do this, it must catalyze investment and innovation that will support sustained growth and give rise to new economic opportunities" (OECD, 2011).

More precisely, a "green recovery" (or "green stimulus") is a macroeconomic stabilization response to a drop in gross domestic product (GDP) in times of recession, which aims first and foremost at replacing the jobs lost by allocating public spending to existing sectors or economic activities that emit few greenhouse gases. Through the creation of "green jobs" (and greening jobs), policymakers seek to minimize the ecological impact of the recovery of employment by relying on existing economic sectors (typically the renewable energy sector, for example, manufacturing solar panels or wind turbines).

Table 5.1 Two shades of green growth

Type of Green growth	Origin / inspiration	Objectives / indicators	Applications / achievements
Green recovery	Green Jobs: Towards Decent Work in a *Sustainable, LowCarbon World*, ILO/UNEP, 24 September 2008	Development of green jobs through eco-activities (waste management, nature conservation, etc.)	The United States during the great depression (1930s)) European Union and United States during the "great recession" (2008–2010)
-	*A Green New Deal*, New Economics Foundation, July 2008 ; *Un «Green New* Deal» pour l'Europe Towards a green modernization in the face of crisis, The Greens-European *Parliament et Wuppertal Institute,* September 2009.	GDP growth via public investments in ecological modernization (energy efficiency; deployment of renewable energy, "green" infrastructures, etc.)	-

"Green growth," on the other hand, is an economic transformation strategy aimed at developing new sources of GDP growth through public investment, for example the hydrogen economy or electric vehicles (some models of circular economy fit here as well, see Table 5.1).

Hence the need to substantially revise the goals and targets of the EU Green Deal to turn it into a Social and Green Deal (Table 5.2 and Table 5.3).

The European Green Deal, as it is, is built on four policy pillars, each with specific goals and indicators (Table 5.2), namely Climate and Energy policy (aiming at Climate neutrality); Resource and Pollution policy (aiming at Material efficiency); Food and Agriculture policy (aiming at Food sovereignty); and Biodiversity and Ecosystems policy (aiming at Natural Conservation). This silo approach to policymaking is not capable, in our view of addressing the many transversal issues of the EGD.

Table 5.2 *The Green Deal, 2030 Targets*

Policy Pillars	**Climate and Energy**	**Resource and Pollution**	**Food and Agriculture**	**Biodiversity and Ecosystems**
Goals	Climate neutrality	Material efficiency	Food sovereignty	Natural Conservation
Indicators	At least 55% decrease in GHG emissions against the 1990 baseline; At least 42.5% of renewable energy in the energy mix (decarbonization of energy) 16% share of renewable fuels in transport (sustainable mobility)	Decrease by 30% in DMC per capita (resource use) against the 2020 baseline At least a 55% decrease in the number of premature deaths from air pollution (PM 2.5) against a 2005 baseline	At least 25% of agricultural land under organic farming (sustainable food) 50% decrease in the use of chemical pesticides (health-environment) with three-year baseline, comprising the average of 2015, 2016, and 2017.	30% of species reaching favorable conservation status (biodiversity) Restore at least 20% of the EU's land and 20% of the EU's seas by 2030 (ecosystems) Halve land artificialization with a 2000–2006 baseline (Soil conservation)

Table 5.3 The Social and Green Deal, 2024 onwards

Policy Pillars	**Climate and Energy**	**Resource and Pollution**	**Food and Agriculture**	**Biodiversity and Ecosystems**
Goals	Climate neutrality + equity	Material efficiency + sufficiency	Food sovereignty + security	Conservation + Regeneration and Protection
Indicators	Green Deal indicators +	Green Deal indicators +	Green Deal indicators +	Green Deal indicators +
	• Ensure fuel equity: cut housing and mobility fuel poverty by half • Ensure global equity: Cut resource extraction outside the EU by 55%; Cut emissions "compensation" outside the EU by 55%	• Provide universal basic services financed by taxing excessive consumption	• Ensure healthy, sustainable, and nutritious food security	• Rewilding • Job guarantee attached to regeneration • Protection from climate and ecological shocks (fires, flooding, etc.)

A transition is needed toward a social-ecological compact able to upgrade the Green Deal in order to guarantee climate neutrality and equity, material efficiency and sufficiency, food sovereignty and security, and finally conservation and Regeneration (Table 5.3).

The rationale of the transformation of the Green Deal into the Social and Green Deal is twofold:

- First, the Green Deal as it stands increases the risk of worsening inequality and social revolt within the EU while missing key environmental targets;
- It also risks alienating the EU's global partners, blocking and even reversing frail progress in environmental policies and global environmental governance (starting with climate negotiations).

Consider the overarching goal of becoming "the first climate-neutral continent" without tackling energy poverty and global inequality. Rising energy costs, unaffordability of home weatherization, and low-carbon equipment prevent most Europeans from actually cutting further their emissions and feed social frustration against environmental norms and standards (such as low emissions areas). The global impact of rare earth extraction and the reliance on inefficient compensation schemes undermine the EU's credibility in climate negotiations.

Consider the goal of material efficiency without material sufficiency: domestic material consumption has hardly been reduced in the EU in the last twenty years[25] while access to essential services such as energy, transport, and digital communication is becoming more difficult[26].

Consider the social and political challenge of widespread food insecurity, which was on the rise in the EU even before the Russian aggression in Ukraine, while farmers and farm workers are socially vulnerable.

Consider, finally, the massive ongoing collapse of ecosystems and biodiversity, which sustains European economies, or the fact that Europeans are already suffering from extreme climate shocks without adequate protection[27].

International cooperation

In the field of international cooperation, the concept of just transition first took concrete form as the Just Transition Transaction (JTT) partnership. This mechanism, backed by a multilateral consortium, seeks to phase out coal in the South African energy mix, in the spirit of the Paris Agreement.[28]

This first partnership had limited scope but was subsequently expanded to take the form of the "Just Energy Transition Partnership" (JETP) announced at COP 26 in Glasgow in November 2021, in the wake of the Just Transition Declaration (see box).

Five donors subsequently granted $8.5 billion to the South African government, which published its JETP investment plan (JETP IP) at the Sharm El Sheikh COP 27 in November 2022. This IP indicated that the JETP could avoid up to 1.5 gigatonnes of greenhouse gas emissions over the next two decades. That same month, a second JETP with Indonesia for $20 billion was signed, followed in December 2022 by a third partnership with Vietnam for $15.5 billion. At the European Union – African Union Summit on February 18, 2022, a proposal was made to establish new partnerships for a just energy transition in Africa, the first one being signed with Senegal.

Energy partnerships for a just transition thus started with a sectoral prototype for a single country but are becoming more comprehensive: they now include all aspects of national energy strategies and are applicable to multiple countries. This can be seen in the "Climate Promise" initiative launched by UNDP, which is helping 34 countries and territories around the world (e.g., Serbia, Costa Rica, and Zimbabwe) to consolidate the principles, processes, and practices of the just transition.

This approach of expanding the just transition so that it is more holistic could continue in five directions:

- On the climate-crisis front, by combining objectives to reduce greenhouse gas emissions with objectives to improve human well-being, starting with employment and health objectives.
- By linking targets to reduce greenhouse gas emissions in developing countries to the acceleration of emission reductions in the OECD countries, the goal of achieving a global just transition can be pursued.
- By expanding the scope of just transition partnerships to include responses to ecological shocks, starting with climate shocks (heat waves, droughts, floods, etc.), in order to reduce the social inequalities they generate.
- By expanding the scope of just transition partnerships to include ecosystem and biodiversity preservation in relation to human well-being, in a relational and non-instrumental approach to natural resources and non-human species as promoted by IPBES.[29]
- By strengthening the participatory dimension of just transition policies, especially by ensuring that the rights of indigenous communities are respected, as promoted by the global strategy of COP 15.[30]

NOTES

1. A possible origin is Chapter 6 of Book IV of John Stuart Mill's Principles of Political Economy where he envisions a "steady-state" economy.
2. Cassiers et al. 2017, p. 2
3. With the subtitle "Measuring progress, true wealth and well-being," the international conference took place on November 19 and 20, 2007 in Brussels, co-organized by the European Commission, the European Parliament, the Club of Rome, the OECD, and the WWF ; notes from the event are available at https://wayback.archive-it.org/org

-1495/20230414094735/https://ec.europa.eu/environment/beyond_gdp/download/bgdp-summary-notes.pdf

4. https://ec.europa.eu/transparency/documents-register/detail?ref=COM(2009)433&lang=en
5. The stated goals of the conference were: "to shift the discourse towards future-oriented economic policymaking and the benefits of beyond-growth indicators for a well-being European economy"; "to shape the EU's path to a more resilient economic agenda in line with the European Green Deal objectives and the Sustainable Development Goals"; to "create real policy impact with new proposals to establish a new social, economic, and environmental contract"; and to "create new and unusual alliances between a great diversity of stakeholders." The follow-up event of the conference, organized in early December 2023, was devoted to transforming the EU Green Deal into a Social and Green Deal https://www.beyond-growth-2023.eu/blueprint-for-a-social-and-green-deal-livestream/ ; these goals were also reflected by the comprehensive companion Joint Research Center publication "Beyond Growth – Pathways towards Sustainable Prosperity in the EU" (European Parliament, 2023).
6. Dahlgren and Whitehead, 1991
7. Link and Phelan, 1995.
8. In the words of the WHO Secretary General: "Health does not begin in clinics or hospitals any more than justice begins in law courts or peace starts on the battlefield. Rather, health starts with the conditions in which we are born and raised, and in schools, streets, workplaces, homes, markets, water sources, kitchens, and in the very air we breathe" (Ghebreyesus, 2023).
9. Commercial determinants of health are "a key social determinant, and refer to the conditions, actions and omissions by commercial actors that affect health" or alternatively "the private sector activities that affect people's health" such as "smoking, air pollution, alcohol use, obesity and physical inactivity" (WHO 2023). As argued by Stegeman et al. (2024): "People's health, wellbeing and levels of health inequalities in societies are determined by a wide range of factors, that are beyond the scope of health care systems. The economy itself is a critical determinant of health, that affects other key determinants, like good quality environments, adequate income, housing, a sense of safety, security and belonging, purpose and participation."
10. See Waldinger and Schulz (2023).
11. One Health High-Level Expert Panel (2022).
12. Lepenies (2016).
13. Chancel et al. (2022).
14. Globally, it is estimated that between 25% and 50% of mortality stems from premature avertable mortality from non-communicable diseases (NCDs), the most common NCDs being responsible for 70% of deaths

globally and driven by four main risk factors: tobacco use, physical inactivity, the harmful use of alcohol, and unhealthy diets (Martinez, Lloyd-Sherlock, Soliz et al., 2020), all of which are "strongly commercially influenced" (WHO 2023). See also Singh and Hickel (2023).

15. Studies have multiplied over the past fifteen years to attest to the increase in social isolation in OECD countries (Office of the Surgeon General, 2023; Berlingieri et al., 2023).
16. IPBES (2019).
17. Pritchett and Summers (1996).
18. Preston (1975) highlights a positive but non-linear relationship between an increase in level of GDP per capita and an increase in life expectancy, strong for "poor" countries (with a low level of GDP per capita) and weak for rich countries. In other words, increases in the standard of living explain changes in life expectancy very poorly: variations of a few thousand dollars per inhabitant lead to leaps in life expectancy of 25 years (from 45 years to 70 years) while considerable gaps in per capita income, from $10,000 to $50,000, translate into relatively modest life expectancy increases (of the order of 5 years). Overall, the correlation between changes in income and changes in life expectancy over 30 years for 30 countries is found to be statistically insignificant.
19. The first mention of this type of methodology in the official documents of the World Health Organization appeared in 1951, only three years only after the creation of WHO, in a working document which recommends the collection and dissemination of "empirical evidence" of potential economic gains associated with public health policies with the explicit goal of persuading governments to allocate more financial resources to these policies).
20. WHO Council on the Economics of Health for All (2023).
21. Eurobarometer, Autumn 2023.
22. "A green transition that leaves no one behind: 88% of EU citizens support this goal. Yet, only 46% of Europeans are currently confident that by 2050 sustainable energy, products, and services will be affordable for everyone, including poorer people."
23. https://www.justtransition.scot/
24. https://www.justtransition.scot/
25. See Eurostat https://ec.europa.eu/eurostat/fr/web/products-eurostat-news/w/ddn-20230731-1#:~:text=In%202022%2C%20the%20domestic%20material,(14.4%20tonnes%20per%20person).
26. See European Commission, 2023 https://ec.europa.eu/social/main.jsp?langId=en&catId=89&furtherNews=yes&newsId=10595
27. See EEA, 2023 https://www.eea.europa.eu/en/analysis/indicators/economic-losses-from-climate-related
28. Steyn et al. (2021).
29. Pascual, Balvanera and Anderson (2023).
30. CBD, 2022.

6. Emerging institutions

Institutions embedding and implementing just transition approaches reviewed in the first two parts of this book are emerging all over the world. The presentation of twelve of them in the following pages dovetails with the chronological evolution of the just transition paradigm: at first narrow and restrictive and then gradually broadening to encompass a wider conception of justice up until the recognition of non-human rights. This part thus starts with the historical origin of the just transition – social compensation of fossil fuel workers in the US – to shift to wider economic issues (income) onto broader human well-being (food, mobility, and housing), then to natural resources, and finally the inclusion of non-human species in the circle of human justice.

JUST TRANSITION IN FOSSIL FUELS INDUSTRIES (US AND EU REGIONS)

When US trade unionist Tony Mazzocchi (Mazzocchi, 1993) introduced the notion of just transition, he referred to a "helping hand" to fossil fuel workers to allow them to make a new start in life in the event of a phase-out of their industry for the sake of climate mitigation[1]. In this perspective, economist Robert Pollin (Pollin, 2023) argues that there are three "critical components" of a just transition policy that take the form of guarantees for workers: "a guaranteed new job; a guaranteed level of pay with their new job that is at least comparable to their previous fossil fuel industry job; a guarantee that their pensions will remain intact regardless of whether their employers' business operations are phased out."

A number of studies show that the financial costs of what Mazzocchi had in mind when he coined the phrase "just transition" are insignificant compared to the total investment necessary for the transition to clean energy. In the United States, Pollin and Callaci (2019) estimate that the cost of income, retraining, and relocation support for workers facing retrenchments, guaranteeing the pensions for workers in the affected industries, and mounting effective transition programs for what are now fossil fuel–dependent communities amount to $600 million per year, or around 1% of the total investment needed to switch the energy system to zero carbon.

Local initiatives of just transition policies understood in this perspective are already taking place. For instance, in the state of Wyoming, coal miners hit by workforce reductions have found new jobs in the growing wind energy sector, and West Virginia, a Just Transition Fund (JTF) has received grants totaling $62.8 million from the US Economic Development Administration and $26 million from non-federal sources. The JTF is part of a broader initiative, the Appalachian Climate Technologies Coalition (ACT Now Coalition), bringing together local actors to secure income, pensions, and training during the transition away from coal.

Such an approach is also developed at the EU level. The COP24 (2018) declaration "Solidarity and Just Transition: Silesia Declaration" (see Box 6.1) has initiated an effort to develop such policies. First released as a Ministerial Declaration, the declaration was adopted by acclamation at the Leaders´ Summit during the 24th Conference of the Parties (COP24) to the United Nations Framework Convention on Climate Change (UNFCCC), on 3 December 2018 in Katowice, Poland.

BOX 6.1 SOLIDARITY AND JUST TRANSITION SILESIA DECLARATION

We, the Heads of State and Government,

Emphasizing that climate change is one of the greatest challenges of our time and a common concern of humankind, and that Parties to the Paris Agreement recognized the need for an effective and progressive response to the urgent threat of climate change on the basis of the best available scientific knowledge;

Stressing that addressing climate change requires a paradigm shift towards building low greenhouse gas emission and climate-resilient economies and societies for all, that offers substantial opportunities and ensure continued high growth and sustainable development, while ensuring a just transition of the workforce that creates decent work and quality jobs;

Reaffirming that Parties to the Paris Agreement on climate change are taking into account the imperatives of a just transition of the workforce and the creation of decent work and quality jobs, in accordance with nationally defined development priorities, and also reaffirming that the Paris Agreement emphasizes the intrinsic relationship that climate change actions, responses, and impacts have with equitable access to sustainable development and the eradication of poverty;

Recognizing the specific needs and special circumstances of developing countries, especially those that are particularly vulnerable to the adverse effects of climate change and the natural disasters and other exogenous shocks, exacerbated by climate change, which bring devastating effects to vulnerable workers and people living in poverty with limited savings and no social safety net, increasing the challenges and the obstacles to a just transition, especially for countries characterized by fragile environmental conditions and least developed countries;

Also recognizing that the circumstances of economic sectors, cities, and regions that are most likely to be affected by the transition vary from country to country depending on their level of development;

Taking note of the importance of the International Labor Organization's "Guidelines for a just transition towards environmentally sustainable economies and societies for all," and its considerations, as appropriate, by Parties while fulfilling their commitments under the Paris Agreement on climate change;

Highlighting that the United Nations 2030 Agenda for Sustainable Development, as well as its Sustainable Development Goals, confirm the need to tackle environmental, social, and economic problems in a coherent and integrated manner;

Stress that just transition of the workforce and the creation of decent work and quality jobs are crucial to ensure an effective and inclusive transition to low greenhouse gas emissions and climate resilient development, and to enhance public support for achieving the long-term goals of the Paris Agreement;

Emphasize that development measures to make infrastructure climate-resilient and enhance institutional capacity in this respect have the potential to be a source of decent job creation for both women and men while improving resilience, especially in vulnerable countries;

Underline employment opportunities that the transition to low-greenhouse gas emission and climate-resilient economies has already created and the potential for the creation of a number of additional jobs as a result of increased global ambition;

Recognize the challenges faced by sectors, cities, and regions in transition from fossil fuels and high-emitting industries, and the importance of ensuring a decent future for workers impacted by the transition, while working to ensure sustainable development and community renewal;

Note the importance of a participatory and representative process of social dialogue involving all social partners to promote high employment rates, adequate social protection, labor standards, and wellbeing of workers and their communities when developing nationally determined contributions, long-term low greenhouse gas emission development strategies, and adaptation planning processes;

Source: UNFCC.

As part of the European Green Deal, the Just Transition Mechanism (JTM) was set up to leave no person and no region behind in the transition towards a climate-neutral economy. It includes the Just Transition Fund (JTF), which will invest €17.5 billion in the 2021–2027 period in the territories most affected by the transition to a climate-neutral economy. The JTF Regulation entered into force on 1 July 2021. Member States are already preparing their territorial Just Transition Plans (TJTP).

The region of Silesia, for instance has the largest hard coal mining industry in the EU and will gradually move away from coal extraction and coal combustion. This will also have an effect on part of Western Małopolska. These regions will therefore receive the majority of funding through the JTF in Poland. With a budget of around €2.4 billion for Silesia and Western Małopolska, this EU funding will assist the regions' inhabitants and support them during the transition to a green economy, with new job opportunities and cleaner air. The Fund will specifically support local economic diversification by investing in small and medium-sized businesses (SMEs) working on renewable energy, clean mobility, and other green sectors. To restore environmental damage from the mining activities, the JTF will also invest in the rehabilitation and decontamination of 2800 ha of post-mining areas in line with the polluter pays principle.

To help reduce energy bills and to allow citizens to benefit from stable, ecological, and affordable energy sources, the Fund will invest in

Western Małopolska in the energy efficiency of public buildings and housing, including by supporting home insulation, rooftop solar installations, and heat pumps.

The JTF will also invest in the training of 100,000 workers, many of whom currently work in the fossil fuels sector, and equip them with new skills to work in renewable and climate-neutral industries. 27,000 new jobs are expected to be created in Silesia directly as a result of the Just Transition Plan measures.

These types of policies are developing in a number of European regions, as is the case with the just transition plan adopted by the Auvergne-Rhône-Alpes region in 2022, aiming at changing the economic model in four key industrial sectors which are large emitters of greenhouse gases: refinery, non-metallic mineral products, chemicals, and metallurgy.

INCOME FOR ECOLOGICAL TRANSITION (SWITZERLAND)

The Income for Ecological Transition (or "Revenu de transition écologique," in short RTE) is a policy tool developed by philosopher and economist Sophie Swaton (University of Lausanne), president and founder of the Zoein Foundation (Swaton, 2018). The key idea of the RTE is to offer monetary support to people who engage, via a dedicated democratic structure, in an activity promoting the ecological transition, such as sustainable food or renewable energy.

The RTE is not a form of universal basic income (UBI), which aims at mitigating poverty by guaranteeing a universal monthly allowance to cover needs without conditions or formalities. The RTE is conditioned on the engagement of people in an ecological transition and/or social activity.

The RTE is thus a system, including monetary compensation and support, offered to people who engage in activities responding to the ecological and social emergencies of their territories and that adhere to a democratic or cooperative structure for ecological transition. Based on the needs, skills, and desires of people, the purpose of the RTE is to enable everyone, including the most vulnerable, to develop a paid, fulfilling activity that allows them to live with dignity, all while respecting planetary boundaries. By being supported, people and ecological transition initiatives can revitalize territories and make our society more resilient.

The RTE has attracted interest in France and Switzerland. In the canton of Vaud, an initiative has been launched to set up an RTE pilot project in 2024, supported by a feasibility study (Fondation Zoein, 2023). This study shows[2] that currently, activities favorable to the ecological transition or compatible with it, that is to say, with a positive impact in terms of reducing the carbon footprint, are rarely present in the economic fabric of the canton of Vaud.

FOOD SOCIAL SECURITY (FRANCE)

According to the FAO, food insecurity occurs when a person lacks regular access to enough safe and nutritious food for normal development and an active and healthy life, which may be due to unavailability of food and/or lack of resources to obtain food (FAO et al. 2023)[3]. Yet food insecurity is also a growing problem for developed countries, especially in countries hit by food inflation both before and after the Russian aggression in Ukraine in February 2022 (that triggered a very sharp increase in food prices, of 20% for instance in France).

Indeed, Eurostat estimated that in 2016 more than 20% of Europeans were unable to afford a meal with meat, fish or a vegetarian equivalent every other day due to low income (Eurostat, 2018), and it has been established that food insecurity rises significantly in EU member states faced with a shock on household income (Davis and Baumberg, 2017).

Recent studies in France estimate that 12% of adults, younger than the general population and mostly women, were in a state of food insecurity in 2014–2015, or around 8 million people, while 7 million people would be affected by food aid in 2020, a significant increase since 2019, when there were 5.5 million people in this situation (CNA, 2022). This proportion has risen with the shock on global food supply chains in February 2021: 16% of French people now say they do not have enough to eat, according to a survey by the Research Center for the Study and Observation of Living Conditions published in May 2023 (Bléhaut et Gressier, 2023)[4].

To alleviate this social emergency, the "food social security" (Sécurité sociale de l'alimentation) project has been publicly supported since 2019 in France by a collective of associations and organizations, and several proposals have emerged in the public debate in the last few years to implement new systems for direct access to quality products[5]:

- The social food budget, up to €150 per month, proposed by Engineers Without Borders, for the purchase of approved products from approved professionals, is financed by a progressive rate and distributed through the "carte vitale," which is used for healthcare services (February 2019);
- Food vouchers for the most deprived, proposed by the citizens' climate convention, would be used in associations for the maintenance of peasant agriculture (AMAP) or for sustainable products, from agroecology and short circuits. Financing would be based on the taxation of "ultra-processed" products with a high carbon footprint and low nutritional intake (June 2020);
- The "ecological solidarity card" proposed by the think tank La Fabrique Écologique would count points when people purchase sustainable products to be used for similar purchases, the list and characteristics of which would be determined with health professionals. The state could supplement this card for low incomes in order to direct consumption towards healthy products (June 2020);
- The "green check" proposed by the think tank Terra Nova of €300 per year per beneficiary for incomes below 1.3 minimum wage, or around 15 million people, is a cost borne by the State in order to finance the purchase of goods and services beneficial to the environment (December 2020).

Many local initiatives have followed these proposals. For instance, in February 2023 in the southern city of Montpellier. The fund relies on shared, differentiated contributions and equal benefits: each of the 450 members contributes each month—between 1 and 150 euros, or more—then all receive the same sum of 100 euros. The amount received is to be spent in specific food distribution locations (farmers' markets, organic and local grocery stores, purchasing groups). To do this, members use Mona, a currency created specifically for the fund.

On April 1, 2024, 400 citizens in the département of Gironde (where 200,000 people are in a situation of food insecurity) engaged in a similar scheme: they contribute to a common fund according to their means, the collected sum being distributed in the form of a financial allocation. In practical terms, 400 citizens living in four rural and urban areas of the département with a third of their inhabitants having low income (Bordeaux, Bègles, South-Gironde, and the Pays Foyen) contribute according to their means (10 euros per month at least) and receive in exchange 150 euros or rather 150 MonA, the local currency for this Social Food Security. This allocation allows them to do their shopping in local and organic grocery stores, small supermarkets or markets, where products that respect short circuits or fair remuneration for farmers are being offered.

A similar scheme was voted by the Paris Council in November 2023 for entry into force in early 2024. The goal, here also, is to mitigate food insecurity while promoting local and environmentally friendly production. Each beneficiary will receive 100 euros to spend in businesses selected for the quality of their supply. As with health insurance, everyone will contribute according to their income, and the city will finance part of it.

COMMON MOBILITY (SPAIN)

In the aftermath of the Russian aggression in Ukraine in February 2022, EU countries saw a dramatic increase in the price of energy (around a 30% increase in the fall of 2022 on average), and energy poverty became the focus of attention for European institutions, with the European Parliament proposing in the summer of 2022 to amend the "Social Climate Fund" of the EU Green Deal (see part 2) to include a definition of energy poverty encompassing not only housing but also mobility[6,].

But member states also decided independently to implement very significant national plans supporting purchasing power by subsidizing energy. France, for instance decided on a 20 billion euros subsidy to lower fuel prices at the gas pump without social criteria. Spain took an alternative approach: subsidizing public transportation.

In response to the energy price crisis, the Spanish government decided to support 30% of the final cost of a newly created multi-journey train ticket launched in September 2022. The state-owned company RENFE, as well as subnational authorities, financially compensated for the implementation of this measure, as well as for regional train and public bus transport subsidies. This measure was part of a larger package encouraging the use of public transport in daily mobility, as a safer, more reliable, more comfortable, more economical and more sustainable than the private car.

The financing of these measures has been articulated through various extraordinary credits charged to the grouped around "Subsidies and support to land transportation" within the General State Budget according to two modalities (Greenpeace, 2023): direct aid to autonomous communities[7] to reduce the price of transport tickets for regular users; and direct aid to local entities for the reduction of ticket price transportation to regular users.

From September 1, 2022, until December 31, 2023 (with a possible extension), important discounts and/or bonuses were allowed both for urban transport and railway (Table 6.1).

Greenpeace estimates that metro ridership during this period was up 17% in cities, and 30% for the bus. The number of trips on the classic regional network jumped by 67%, and 64% for high-speed networks. As for peri-urban networks, their use increased by 27%. In parallel, these measures have led to a drop of 160 to 320 tons of CO_2 emissions per day in the country.

LOCAL ENERGY COMMUNITIES (EU)

According to Bonfert (2024), energy communities involve public, private, or community actors in co-producing and distributing renewable energy. They are often praised for helping democratize, decentralize, and socially embed the energy system but remain constrained by economic and legal barriers. Energy communities are, in practical terms, citizen-driven collectives engaged in low-carbon energy transition. They are emerging just transition institutions in two respects: first, they aim at making renewable energy more accessible and secure; they also aim at

Table 6.1 Subsidized collective transportation in Spain

Mode of transport	Service	Period 1: from September 1, 2022, to December 31	Period 2: from January 1, 2023, to December 31, 2023 to 31 December 2023
Urban transport	Subway Bus	30% multi-trip passes and tickets	50% multi-trip passes and tickets
Rail	Suburban trains or regional rail network Journeys of less than 100 minutes on the national high-speed network	Free (recurring users) 50% multi-trip passes and tickets	Free (recurring users) 50% multi-trip passes and tickets

Source: Greenpeace, 2023.

making social-ecological policy more democratic via the active participation of citizens.

Through the Clean Energy for All Europeans package, the EU introduced the concept of energy communities in its legislation, notably as citizen energy communities and renewable energy communities. Under EU law, energy communities can take the form of any legal entity, including an association, a cooperative, a partnership, a non-profit organization, or a limited liability company.

More specifically, the Directive on common rules for the internal electricity market (EU/2019/944) introduced new rules to enable active consumer participation, individually or through citizen energy communities, in all markets, by generating, consuming, sharing, or selling electricity, or by providing flexibility services through demand-response and storage.

There are today three major frequent business models for energy communities according to the European Commission:

- Generation and supply: Supply of electricity and gas sourced from external local producers through Power Purchase Agreements, wholesale markets, or community-owned production capacity to their customers.
- Collective investments in production installations: In collective investments, consumers pay a fixed membership fee or a variable stake to become members of an energy community that acts as an energy producer. Power Purchase Agreements are often in place within cooperative investments to cover the produced energy and related financial products, like green certifications or guarantees of origin.
- Collective self-consumption: They link energy consumers and producers in the same area. As national regulation highly influences them, members' ability to sell their electricity to other community members and to make use of offsetting mechanisms of the electricity meters might change from country to country.

As Lakeman (2024) explains, local energy communities (LECs) are emerging in European member states at the municipal level under these various forms, "comprising stakeholders ranging from households to local government"[8]. Wierling et al. (2023) argue that at least 2 million people "invested their time, creativity, and money" into the installation of about 10 GW of renewable capacity for a total of 10,000 initiatives and 16,000 production units in 29 countries.

SOCIAL-ECOLOGICAL ARCHITECTURE (AFRICA)

The Lancet Commission studying the relationships between urban spaces, health, and sustainability [Giles-Corti et al., 2022] recommends, with supporting evidence, compact cities with higher density, adapted to pedestrians and cyclists, and precisely identifies "eight integrated urban systems policies" that work together to create eight centers of intervention:

- Three of these policies concern regional planning (accessibility of destinations; distribution of employment; management of demand to reduce car driving).
- Five concern local urban planning (design of travel networks adapted to pedestrians and cyclists; optimization of residential density; reduction of distance to public transport; increase in the diversity of housing and mixed land uses; improvement of the attractiveness of active modes of transport).

This new design of urban spaces needs to be accompanied by new ways to build, encompassing new visions of architecture, more socially useful and materially sober.

Architect Francis Kéré was born in 1965 in Burkina Faso, the eldest son of the village chief and the first in his community to go to school. The small classroom of his childhood in Tenkodogo was built of cement blocks and lacked ventilation and light.

His first and most iconic achievement to date is the Gando primary school, which served as a matrix for his work and to which he later added a complex of housing for teachers and a library. There, Kéré understood that a seemingly simple objective, namely allowing children to go to school comfortably, had to be at the heart of his architectural project, which combines double roofs, thermal mass, wind towers, indirect lighting, cross ventilation, and shading chambers (instead of conventional windows, doors, and columns).

The success earned him the Aga Khan Award for Architecture in 2004 and was the catalyst for establishing his practice, Kéré Architecture, in Berlin (Germany) in 2005. The creation of primary, secondary, post-secondary, and medical education quickly followed across Burkina Faso, Kenya, Mozambique, and Uganda. He has since tackled a project for the National Assembly of Benin, which will soon see the light of day, and the National Assembly of Burkina Faso. His buildings, combining ecological sobriety and social utility, are designed and erected for and with the human communities and the environment where they stand at each step of the way, as with the new parliament of the Republic of Benin, inspired by the palaver tree, the age-old West African tradition of meeting under a tree to make consensual decisions in the interest of a community. The same goes for the proposal for a new National Assembly of Burkina Faso, a monumental stepped pyramidal structure, the outer shell of which offers a unique public gathering space in the heart of the capital Ouagadougou[9].

URBAN JUST ADAPTATION (BANGKOK, THAILAND)

Thailand faces high exposure to natural hazard risks (ranked 81st out of 191 countries by the 2019 Inform Risk Index)[10] and Bangkok is one of the most vulnerable cities in the world when it comes to climate change: the World Bank estimated that it faces a risk of 40 percent inundation by extreme rainfall as early as 2030[11] (the 2011 floods, the worst in half a century, inundated the city for almost three months, resulting in 800 people dead and an overall cost of 40 billion US dollars). On the other hand, Marks and Connell (2023) show that "the intensity of Bangkok's urban heat island during the dry season can be as high as 6–7°C and in the densest areas the urban heat island's intensity is approximately 4°C … causing a city already oppressively hot to become even hotter."

These authors also show how the urban heat island (due to the lack of green space, high levels of air conditioning, and high rates of vehicle exhaust fumes) is "highly unequal and unjust": "those who contribute to and profit the most from Bangkok's urban heat island, such as real estate developers, shopping mall owners, and automobile corporations, suffer the least from its effects, whereas low-income communities hardly contribute to this problem, yet are the most vulnerable."

Against this backdrop of extreme flood and heat risk, landscape architect Kotchakorn Voraakhom has developed new urban adaptation projects focused on mitigating both climate impact and the inequality stemming from it.

Her hallmark design, Chulalongkorn Centenary Park, opened in 2017 on 11 acres of property in the heart of Bangkok, is the first critical piece of green infrastructure in Bangkok to reduce urban flood risk. With on-site water management, the park can collect, treat, and hold up to one million gallons of water, alleviating overwhelmed public sewage systems during heavy rainfall. In addition to being Bangkok's first park in 30 years, it was also the first city public park led by a female landscape architect. In dry periods, up to a million gallons is available for watering. By sitting on a 3-degree angle, Chulalongkorn Centenary Park collects rainwater from its green roof, which can slow down runoff up to 20 times more than regular concrete surfaces.

Some of the water is stored in underground tanks, and the rest is sent through a series of ecological components, including a detention lawn and wetlands, which filter, aerate, and purify the water. Finally, the water flows down to the retention pond--capable of doubling in size to handle severe floods--where it completes the cycle, now available for irrigation and distribution to surrounding facilities.

Another Kotchakorn project is Chong Nonsi Canal Park, situated above a major canal now reconnected to fresh water to nourish greenery on parkland. Like many waterways, this one had been disconnected from the canal network, leaving it stagnant and polluted. Kotchakorn's group is working with community leaders to help rehouse families being displaced as authorities plan to widen canals to move floodwaters through faster within the "Landprocess[12] and Porous City Network" to build innovative landscape solutions for urban resilience in Bangkok.

Landprocess helps vulnerable neighborhoods most at risk of flooding and displacement from rising sea levels better understand climate impacts. Landprocess collaborates with these communities to design solutions to address these challenges, enabling them to successfully put forward their projects for governmental approval and funding. This currently includes 750 households most at risk of flooding at the Latprao Canal community, 800 others at the Hat-Lek Fishery community who are affected by rising sea levels, and 300 households at Bann-Pai who were affected by living in the floodplain.

Through Landprocess' participatory design process, women--as the main caretakers of the family and first-hand witnesses of issues in their communities--have provided detailed insights and ideas highly useful in creating sustainable designs catered to improving the quality of life and social fabric of their society. Landprocess repurposed wasted rooftop space to address food and water scarcity in preparation for future climate challenges, such as The Thammasat Urban Rooftop Farm, opened in

2019, now Asia's biggest, repurposed 236,806 sq. ft. of abandoned concrete roof space to grow crops.

DISASTER RISK REDUCTION (SOUTH ASIA)

In March 2022, UN Secretary-General Antonio Guterres launched the "Early Warnings for All" initiative, which called for every person on Earth to be protected by early warning systems by 2027. The first "pillar" of this strategy is "Disaster risk knowledge," led by United Nations International Strategy for Disaster Reduction (UNDRR, see Box 6.2).

BOX 6.2 THE DISASTER RISK KNOWLEDGE

Risk knowledge represents the first foundational pillar of effective early warning systems. However, significant gaps in terms of risk information and assessments persist worldwide. Less than half of the countries with existing early warning systems have access to appropriate disaster risk information, and even fewer have national legislation and regulatory frameworks for emergency response.

To address this, Pillar 1 aims to enhance global risk knowledge and integrate it into inclusive, accessible, and effective early warning systems. Activities under Pillar 1 will focus on strengthening the production, access, dissemination, and use of risk information; fostering stronger stakeholder coordination; promoting innovation; and empowering decision-makers and vulnerable communities to understand, identify, and respond to risks.

Source: UNDRR.

South Asia (a region that includes Bangladesh, India, Maldives, Nepal, Pakistan, and Sri Lanka) is home to 20% of the world's population and is one of the world's most disaster-prone regions, combining ecological and social vulnerability (biospheric exposure and social sensitivity). In recent decades, disasters have indeed surged in the region in frequency and intensity (earthquakes, floods, and droughts to avalanches, glacial lake outburst floods, and cyclones), with two-thirds of a hydro-meteorological nature, which the climate crisis is sure to further increase in frequency, severity, and unpredictability of[13].

Under the Sendai Framework for Disaster Risk Reduction 2015–2030, which aims first and foremost at reducing the number of deaths and missing persons linked to disasters worldwide and the number of people affected, including by injury, sickness, damage to habitations, or disruptions to livelihoods, new warning tools combining advanced technology[14] and social awareness and communication are being developed and have proven successful.

According to the World Meteorological Organization, so-called "Multi-hazard early warning systems (MHEWS)" are a "proven, effective and feasible climate adaptation measure that saves lives and provides at least a tenfold return on investment." Recent studies have defined efficient early warning systems as a combination of "risk knowledge, monitoring and prediction, dissemination, and response capability" that "play a crucial role in disaster preparedness and response activities, saving lives, reducing damage, and enhancing community resilience by sharing timely information with vulnerable communities" in South Asia (Morshed et al. 2024)[15]. For instance, India's Central Water Commission (CWC) issues 6000 flood forecasts with over 90% consistent accuracy, disseminating warnings through various social media platforms.

According to WMO (2023), countries with limited to moderate MHEWS coverage have a nearly six-times-higher disaster-related mortality ratio compared with that in countries with substantial to comprehensive coverage (4.05 mortality per 100,000 population, compared with 0.71). Similarly, countries with limited to moderate MHEWS coverage have nearly five times more disaster-affected people than countries with substantial to comprehensive coverage (3,132 compared with 688).

JUST CONSERVATION OF THE AMAZON FOREST (SOUTH AMERICA)

The Amazon forest is a key ecosystem of the Biosphere which is currently on the brink of collapse, with immense global and regional consequences on the balance (Flores et al. 2024). Yet this degradation is not inevitable, and it has actually been reversed between 2004 and 2012 thanks to two key actions.

Environment Minister Marina Silva implemented the Action Plan for the Prevention and Control of Deforestation in the Legal Amazon (PPCDAm) — a program that achieved an 83% decrease in deforestation between 2004 and 2012 in the Brazilian Amazon[16] with a mix of restrictions and incentives, such as the Bolsa Floresta[17]. While deforestation progressed again after her tenure (carbon emissions in the Amazon increased from 240 million tonnes on average from 2010 to 2018 to 440 million in 2019 (+83%) and 520 million in 2020 (+117%)), Silva relaunched a new version of the program in April 2023 (Box 6.3).

BOX 6.3 THE 2023 PPCDAM

1. **Sustainable productive activities**

- Strengthening the bioeconomy
- Application of sustainable management and recuperation of degraded areas
- Dialogue with the 9 states of the Legal Amazon

2. **Environmental oversight and control**
Effective accountability for crimes and violations against the environment

- Improvements in the monitoring of destruction and its chains
- Prevention of destruction
- Coordination with the 9 states of the Legal Amazon

3. **Land and Territorial Planning**
Protection of undesignated public lands

- Expansion and streamlined management of currently protected areas.
- Improvement of the Rural Environmental Registry System (SICAR)
- Large enterprises are aligned with the goal of zero deforestation by 2030.

4. **Normative and Economic Instruments**

- New normative and economic instruments to contain deforestation

Source: Ministry of Environment and Climate Change.

In parallel to these efforts, the rights of indigenous communities have been upheld and strengthened with resounding success. In its overall assessment, IPBES (2019) also emphasizes the fact that the degradation of biodiversity and ecosystems is generally less rapid in territories managed by indigenous peoples than in others. This is particularly true of a strategic territory of the biosphere, the Amazon forest, where deforestation has been visibly less tangible for twenty years on lands controlled by indigenous communities.

Researchers brought together under the aegis of the Red Amazónica de Información Socioambiental Georreferenciada (RAISG) undertook to compare the ecological effect of different territorial management regimes and noted on this subject: "Protected areas. (PA) and indigenous territories (TA) are essential to protect the Amazon. Between the two regimes (PA and TA), about half (48%) of the Amazon is covered... most of the deforestation (86%) took place outside the PA and TA."

These just transitions policies in favor of indigenous communities counter the common perception of conservation policies: It is not a question of preserving ecosystems against the human communities that depend on them but of preserving the social-ecological relationships which are the only ones capable of preventing the Amazon from falling into "savannization," whose global consequences would be considerable. Local just transition meets global just transition.

This observation is even more general: numerous works show that "equitable conservation," which fully recognizes the role of indigenous peoples and indigenous communities, is the most promising way to preserve biodiversity and ecosystems. Conversely, conservation approaches imposed from the outside and which aim to protect natural resources while ignoring the social-ecological relationships that have developed between humans and other species are not only unfair but also ineffective (Dawson et al., 2021; FAO et al., 2021). Thus, the project aiming to conserve 30% of land and maritime surfaces by 2030, today supported by the United Nations (30 by 30), is the subject of criticism from indigenous movements, who fear mass expulsions in the territories concerned in the name of protecting biodiversity.

Indigenous peoples contribute to the improvement and maintenance of biodiversity and wild and domesticated landscapes because they practice agricultural methods adapted to local conditions and compatible with the conservation of biodiversity. They do this by creating habitats rich in species and a great diversity of ecosystems in cultural landscapes and by identifying useful plants and their cultivation in very diverse ecosystems (such as the garden-forests of Indonesia). The ecological challenges are considerable: more than a third of the remaining intact forests on the planet – crucial for the preservation of the climate and biodiversity – are located on the lands of indigenous peoples (Fa et al., 2020).

WATER JUSTICE (CAPE TOWN, SOUTH AFRICA)

South Africa has one of the most progressive constitutions when it comes to the recognition of environmental rights (Box 6.4).

BOX 6.4 SOUTH AFRICA CONSTITUTION, EXTRACTS, 1996

Firstly, the values of the Constitution include those of human dignity, the achievement of equality, and the advancement of human rights and freedoms.

Secondly, the Constitution states that everyone has the right to an environment that is not harmful to their health or well-being; and to have the environment protected, for the benefit of present and future generations, through reasonable legislative and other measures that i) prevent pollution and ecological degradation, ii) promote conservation, and iii) secure ecologically sustainable development and use of natural resources while promoting justifiable economic and social development.

Thirdly, the Constitution states that everyone has the right to have access to sufficient food and water.

Fourthly, the Constitution states that the property clause may not impede the state from taking measures to achieve land, water, and related reform, to redress the results of past racial discrimination.

Source: South Africa Constitution.

Yet, the South African government (DWS, 2019) recognized that the daily reality is far from those principles, with over 3 million people not have access to a basic water supply service and 14.1 million people not have access to safe sanitation[18]. From 1994 on, water governance in South Africa relied mostly on a pricing system known as "block tariffs" whereby "medium users should cover the costs of themselves and the poorest, while high-end users would also pay for the cost of new water sources." The water crisis that hit Cape Town in the mid-2010s put front and center the question of water rationing (Enqvist and Ziervogel, 2019).

From 2015 to 2018, Cape Town experienced a long drought, which threatened to deprive 4 million people of access to drinking water. After the start of the decade marked by heavy rains, the 2015–2016 period saw a drop in precipitation of almost 75%. The city's water reserves (mainly six storage dams) found themselves at a critical threshold: the overall dam levels supplying Cape Town dropped from 92.5% to 23% (Nhamo and Agyepong, 2019).

Gradual responses were implemented to address the increasingly severe water crisis. From 2016, drinking water consumption restrictions of 20% have been applied, but the agricultural sector (highly dependent on irrigation, high withdrawal) is not affected. In July 2017, daily use was reduced to 87 liters per person per day by the city of Cape Town, which imposed further restrictions while raising tariffs. On 4 October 2017, the municipal Department of Safety and Security released a "Critical Water Shortages Disaster Plan" that laid out a "Water Augmentation Plant" but also a 3-phase plan regulating demand (Box 6.5).

BOX 6.5 THE CRITICAL WATER SHORTAGES DISASTER PLAN OF CAPE TOWN, 2017

1. Phase 1 – Preservation Restrictions

Phase 1 requires the implementation of water rationing through pressure management and limited supply to remain within the collective daily water usage of 450 million liters, as per the National Department of Water and Sanitation's required savings of 45% for urbanized areas.

Whilst a minimum level of supply is being maintained for as many informal settlements as possible and critical services such as clinics and hospitals are largely unaffected, there is limited supply across other parts of the city. Furthermore, the city is intensifying its installation of water management devices to limit the consumption of users who are exceeding the current Level 6B water restrictions.

2. Phase 2 – Disaster Restrictions 'Day Zero'

In Phase 2, the City will need to actively assume control over the daily water supply available to households and businesses and ration water in order to maintain human life and critical services, as well as prevent the water disaster from escalating to Phase 3.

In order to keep essential services and vital industry running, the City has calculated that at 13.5% dam storage, Day Zero will take effect. Day Zero is the day when the municipality takes control of the municipal water supply in a phased approach in order to stretch this supply until the dams are at a sufficient level to allow water to be distributed via the reticulation system once again.

Where feasible, some key areas will be prioritized to stay connected during Phase 2. Critical infrastructure, population density, and risk profile for disease outbreak are some of the factors that the City will take into account to decide which areas stay connected.

3. Phase 3 – Full-scale Disaster Implementation

Phase 3 is an extreme disaster scenario in which dam water storage in the WCWSS has been completely depleted. There will be a finite time period during which the City can access water from its reservoirs and reticulation system. The City will prioritize the security of these reservoirs, as any remaining water will be considered an emergency supply until augmented supplies come on stream. Non-surface drinking water supplies, sourced from groundwater abstraction from various aquifers and spring water, will be available for drinking purposes only. The City will distribute this water, supplemented by bottled water, to residents through water collection points with the purpose of maintaining a lifeline drinking supply.

Although the Cape Town water management strategy, which relied on communicating straightforwardly the possibility of extreme water rationing, was hailed as a success because of the reduction in water consumption it triggered, it was also criticized for its lack of inclusiveness. Moreover, a recent study argues that "water crises such as the Day Zero drought in Cape Town are also a product of the unsustainable practices of the elite brought about by the uneven power dynamics of the city"[19] (Savelli, Mazzoleni, and Baldassarre, 2023).

While 16 April 2018 was supposed to be Day Zero (when the dam levels that supply the city's water would hit 13.5%), leading to measures to be enforced in Phase 3, it was later pushed back and eventually canceled. Yet very severe restrictions took place in January and February 2018: water use was limited to 50 liters per person per day, and strict tariffs applied, yet the city maintained its social tariff, providing 10.5 m3 per month at no charge to the approximately 270,000 residential properties and free water through public standpipes to a further 180,000 households living in informal settlements (Ziervogel, 2019).

Many insights can be drawn from the water crisis in Cape Town, the first being that water governance[20] is key to any water crisis (Enqvist and Ziervogel, 2019) and that justice issues cannot be separated from water governance. In fact, in the aftermath of the Cape Town crisis emerged a new National Water and Sanitation Master Plan for South Africa centered on three goals:

- Provide universal and equitable access to reliable water supply and sanitation services.
- Protect, manage, and develop the nation's water resources in a manner that supports justifiable and ecologically sustainable economic and social development.
- Transform access to water to redress the racial imbalances created by apartheid.

These insights are all the more important as many cities will face water shortages in the coming years. In the spring of 2024, the cities of Lima and Mexico City experienced similar situations. The water crisis in Mexico City, home to nearly 22 million people, was such that public authorities expressed concerns that a "day zero" scenario might unfold, where there would not be enough water to meet residents' needs[21]. In Lima, home to 70% of the population in Peru facing a population explosion and the multiplication of longer, more intense, and more frequent episodes of drought, one and a half million inhabitants do not have access to drinking water and most residents depended in the spring of 2024 on the passage of tank trucks.

MULTI-SPECIES JUSTICE (US)

Humans have become masters in the art of collaborating with animals to exploit and profit from other forms of life, such as hunting dogs, fishing cormorants, and even fish-hunting dolphins. But it is also possible to cooperate with non-human species, granting them rights, to improve human well-being. The example of the conflict between environmental activists and forestry industries over the preservation of the spotted owl in the early 1990s in the United States can shed light on this path. In 1990, the spotted owl living in the forests of the northwest United States was designated a "protected species" and placed under the protection of the Endangered Species Act of 1973, one of the most protective and innovative pieces of legislation in the world, limiting, in this respect cases the cutting of trees within a 2km radius around owl nests.

Logging companies threatened imminent bankruptcy and tens of thousands of destroyed jobs and put pressure on local politicians, but federal judges decided to maintain the obligation to preserve the ecosystem to protect the species. Thirty years later, not only have the spotted owl and the forests they inhabit been preserved, but the logging industry itself is on a more viable trajectory as its unsustainable logging has slowed. The spotted owl has shown the way to the preservation of a vast ecosystem and the economic activities associated with it. By choosing to cooperate with her, humans have gained on social and environmental grounds.

This little ball of feathers got the better of the desire to destroy the Crémade woods in Saïx, in Tarn.

For a few days, she had been fluttering and wandering in the woods. Then she began to go back and forth, holding moss and feathers in her beak. Opponents of the A69 Toulouse-Castres motorway project then documented what they were impatiently waiting for: a pair of blue tits was building their nest in one of the oak trees that they had been defending for weeks.

However, this species has been protected since 1981, explains Maxime Zucca, an ornithologist. It is therefore prohibited to disturb it during its reproductive period "provided that the disturbance calls into question the proper completion of [its] biological cycles," according to the decree of October 29, 2009.

On March 22, the French Biodiversity Office (OFB) confirmed that this wood was indeed an area of high environmental concern with proven nesting, prohibiting any felling. The Crémade woods are therefore saved from clearing... at least until September 1st.

The French Biodiversity Office has decided: the Crémade woods are a "non-declassified area with high environmental concerns," which prohibits the cutting of its trees until September 1st. A symbolic victory for opponents of the A69 who are fighting against a highly contested motorway project.

Non-human legal persona (New Zealand)

The Earth Law movement has embraced a holistic approach whereby ecosystems and non-human species, up to biogeochemical cycles, are given rights related to the role they play in maintaining life on Earth. The movement was inspired by a seminal article by Stone (1972) published with the explicit intention to influence Supreme Court justices who were deliberating on the Sierra Club v. Morton decision[22]. In his dissent, Justice Douglas wrote that "Contemporary public concern for protecting nature's ecological equilibrium should lead to the conferral of standing upon environmental objects to sue for their own preservation."

But the tradition of granting non-humans legal rights is much older and is related to the indigenous stream of environmental justice (see Part 1).

Ecuador was the first country in this vein to recognize constitutional rights to Nature as a whole in 2008 (Under "Rights of nature," Article 71 states: Nature, or Pacha Mama, where life is reproduced and occurs, has the right to integral respect for its existence and for the maintenance and regeneration of its life cycles, structure, functions, and evolutionary processes; All persons, communities, peoples, and nations can call upon public authorities to enforce the rights of nature. To enforce and interpret these rights, the principles set forth in the Constitution shall be observed, as appropriate; The State shall give incentives to natural persons and legal entities and to communities to protect nature and to promote respect for all the elements comprising an ecosystem). The Constitucional Tribunal later translated these provisions into legal decisions, especially in the Los Cedros case, where the court blocked a mine project in a protected forest, considering that the natural rights were violated.

The growing recognition throughout the world of the rights inherent to rivers is part of this movement. New Zealand was the first country to recognize rights for the Whanganui River, for which the Iwi tribe had been fighting since 1870.

In March 2017, through the Te Awa Tupua Act, the river was given "rights, powers, duties, and liabilities of a legal person" and assigned two "guardians" responsible for maintaining the river's "health and well-being." According to the new legislation, the river is a living being "running from the mountains to the sea, including its tributaries and all of its physical and metaphysical elements." (New Zealand Ministry of Justice, 2017).

Hence, the rights and interests of Whanganui can be defended in court, where it will be represented by a member of the tribe and another from the government, and complaints can even be filed in its name. What is more, the Iwi tribe was compensated by the New Zealand government with 52 million euros in legal costs and 30 million euros for the protection of the river.

Other countries have since followed suit (the United States through the municipal ordinances taken in around ten states for aquatic ecosystems; in Canada through the adoption of two municipal resolutions concerning the Magpie River; in India, Brazil, and Colombia through jurisprudence; and in Corsica through the declaration of Tavignanu River rights in July 2021).

NOTES

1. "We need to provide workers with a guarantee that they will not have to pay for clean air and water with their jobs, their living standards, or their future" (Mazzochi, 1993).
2. Fondation Zoein (2023).
3. The FAO distinguishes between people experiencing moderate food insecurity (who have reduced the quality and/or quantity of their food and are uncertain about their ability to obtain food due to lack of money or other resources; moderate food insecurity can increase the risk of some forms of malnutrition, such as stunting in children, micronutrient deficiencies, or obesity in adults) and people experiencing severe food insecurity (who have run out of food and, at the most extreme, have gone days without eating).
4. The share of individuals declaring that they do not eat enough increased from 12% to 16% from July to November 2022. Young adults (under 40) are the people most often in quantitative food insufficiency (24%).
5. https://securite-sociale-alimentation.org/
6. Households affected by energy poverty due to housing would be those in the lowest income deciles whose energy expenditure exceeds double the median ratio between energy expenditure and disposable income after the deduction of housing costs. In contrast, those affected by energy poverty due to mobility would be households with a high share

of mobility expenditure relative to disposable income or limited availability of affordable public or alternative modes of transport necessary to meet essential socio-economic needs. In light of this common definition, the Member States would be expected to report to the European authorities on their actions to stem the phenomenon at the national level, while part of the already largely undersized financial resources from the "Social Climate Fund" is supposed to contribute to this at the European level.

7. Autonomous Communities (Comunidades autónomas) are the first level of administrative division in Spain.
8. The most advanced projects have been developed in Amersfoort (Netherlands), Malmö (Sweden), Mechelen (Belgium), and West Suffolk (United Kingdom).
9. For more on these designs, see https://www.kerearchitecture.com/
10. World Bank, 2021.
11. Bangkok sits at only 0.5 to 1.5 m above sea level.
12. Landprocess focuses on increasing carbon-sequestering landscapes such as urban forests, environmentally productive parks, green roofs, and wetlands, and redesigning the waste spaces and infrastructure of concrete cities to return to their natural porosity, increase public health, and urban adaptability.
13. In Pakistan, record-breaking rain in July and August 2022 led to extensive flooding resulting in at least 1,700 deaths, and 33 million people were affected, while almost 8 million people were displaced. Total damage and economic losses were assessed at US$ 30 billion (WMO, 2023).
14. Such as the Disaster Monitoring and Response System (DMRS) that was used to monitor a series of tropical cyclones that formed in the ASEAN region between May and November 2020.
15. To be effective, an Early Warning System must be: Multi-Hazard: it is designed to detect different hazards that may occur alone, simultaneously, or in a cascade; End-to-end: the system covers the entire range, from hazard detection to action, which includes providing understandable and actionable warning messages; and most importantly, People-centered: this means designing the systems with people in mind, to empower

   them to act on time and in an appropriate manner to reduce potential harm (United Nations Office for Disaster Risk Reduction and World Meteorological Organization, 2023).
16. According to the Brazilian government, while in 2004 annual forest loss reached 27,700 km2, by 2012 this figure had been reduced to 4,500 km2.

17. The Bolsa Floresta (translated from Portuguese, this means 'forest allowance') program encompasses a set of integrated interventions aimed at conserving forests and improving the welfare of residents in selected sustainable development reserves (SDRs) of the state of Amazonas in the Brazilian Amazon. Only 1 of the 15 conservation units where Bolsa Floresta is working is a certified REDD+ initiative (Juma), while the other 14 are in the REDD+ readiness phase. The program was started in 2007 and contains a financial compensation program, where a small economic incentive of BRL 50 per month (USD 30) is paid to households for their commitment to zero net deforestation (Source: UN REDD+).
18. "88% of households had access to at least a basic water supply, 76% had access to water in the house or yard, and 12% had access to a public standpipe within 200 m walking distance from home. When minimum standards for reliability of water supply services are taken into account, the percentage of households served drops to 74%. What is more, 79% of households benefitted from at least basic sanitation services. ". When it comes to the state of water resources, more than 50% of South Africa's wetlands have been lost, and of those that remain, 33% are in poor ecological condition. Only 5% of agricultural water used is by black farmers, and 41% of municipal water does not generate revenue." (DWS, 2019).
19. The authors note that "Despite representing only 1.4% and 12.3% of the total population, respectively, elite and upper-middle-income groups together use more than half (51%) of the water consumed by the entire city (Fig. 2b). Informal dwellers and lower-income households constitute together 61.5% of Cape Town's population but consume a mere 27.3% of the city's water."
20. Water governance arrangements are "the set of political, social, economic, and administrative systems that formally and informally control decision-making around water resources development and management" (Enqvist and Ziervogel, 2019).
21. As with Cape Town, several factors contribute to Mexico City's water crisis: over-extraction of groundwater, insufficient water distribution and treatment infrastructure, pollution of water sources, and the effects of climate change, such as changing water regimes, precipitation, and increased frequency of droughts.
22. Brought to prevent the Disney development of the Mineral King Valley in Sequoia National Park.

7. Conclusion: Accelerating just transitions

Our worsening ecological crises reveal a striking paradox of knowledge and action: the considerable progress achieved in environmental sciences over the past three decades brings ever-worse news about the state of the biosphere. The more we become aware of and knowledgeable about our ecological predicament, the more it worsens before our eyes. At least three hypotheses can be considered to shed light on this concerning inconsistency.

The first is that we simply know much more about the problem. The quality of our measuring instruments has dramatically improved and informs us much better than before about the real state of environmental crises that have been neglected for too long; the second, less obvious, is the distance that can form between what we know and what we believe: according to French philosopher Jean-Pierre Dupuy, if we know way more than in the past, we do not yet believe enough in what we now know.

The last hypothesis, which I favor, is that we do not yet know everything we should know, particularly on a crucial question: how to reform human systems to preserve the natural systems on which they depend. If the natural and physical sciences alert us to the reality of ecological crises, they do not give us the means to transform attitudes and behaviors in human societies that are responsible for global environmental change causing the ongoing collapse of the Biosphere. For instance, while climate science has made giant strides in the last decade alone, progress in what might be called "transition science" is much more limited. In short, we know far more about the causes of the climate crisis than about the practical ways to solve it.

Likewise, ocean specialists, the seat of what is shaping up to be one of the most serious environmental crises of our time (not a distant future), pointed precisely to this missing link in ecological knowledge more than a decade ago: "technical means to achieve solutions for many of these problems [affecting the oceans, particularly their acidification] already exist, but...current societal values prevent humanity from addressing them effectively. Overcoming these obstacles is core to the fundamental changes needed to achieve a sustainable and equitable future" (Rogers and Laffoley, 2011). The state of seas and oceans has since then significantly worsened (IOC-UNESCO, 2024).

This book advances, in this regard a simple but powerful idea: human behaviors and attitudes can evolve for the better, provided the essential human social principle, justice, is put at the center of transition policies and institutions.

A certain number of behaviors have direct and indirect consequences on the environment: production, consumption, transportation, nutrition, etc. These behaviors are under the influence of the price system, and more precisely relative prices: if gasoline and domestic fuel oil are relatively inexpensive, households may want to live in peripheral urban areas that are hard to reach and in housing that is difficult to heat. These expenses, and the behaviors of which they are the symptoms, are economically bearable if the price of energy remains moderate.

If public authorities decide to attempt to reform these behaviors effectively, they will have to gradually increase the price of energy while allowing households to opt for other, more environmentally favorable choices, leading to a reduction in greenhouse gas emissions (by subsidizing electric cars or housing retrofits, for example). Two parameters then come into play: the "signal" sent must be sufficiently strong, that is to say, it must induce real changes in behavior (which supposes, for example, setting a price per ton of CO2 at such a level that it will indeed affect individual decisions). But public authorities should also pay attention to the effective capacity of citizens to respond to this price signal by offering alternative options (the so-called "elasticity" or the lack thereof in economic behaviors then comes into play). It is, in any case a change in behavior that is sought, that is to say, a rational response of economic agents to an alteration of the price system by public authorities.

The question of attitudes towards environmental predicaments and how to mitigate them is of a different nature. While behaviors mostly depend on the price system, attitudes depend on the value system. If public authorities want to change not just behaviors but attitudes, they will have to deploy different tools than market-based ones.

Of course, this may not be necessary: by changing prices and modifying behaviors, values could gradually be gradually altered for the better, and ultimately attitudes changed (for instance, when people pay a fee for plastic bags, they might entirely abandon the idea of buying them). However, this is unlikely: attitudes determine behaviors, not the other way around. To ensure the transition takes place, public authorities must therefore develop both a "price policy" and a "value policy." In both policies, justice takes center stage: it is needed for the price policy not to be unjust and for the value policy to be effective.

The power of attitudes is in fact such that most transactions actually take place outside the market, that is to say, outside the price system. For example, the exchange of interpersonal trust, which falls under what Kenneth Arrow called "invisible institutions" and allows economic transactions within the broad ensemble of social transactions, is not reducible to the quest for personal interest and rational choice. Yet trust, invisible and priceless, plays a central role in economic transactions and even more generally in the proper functioning of democracies (Laurent, 2019). A value policy is thus much more powerful than a price policy.

But it is much more difficult to change values than prices – and it is also more questionable. Political regimes that claim to impose values on citizens against their will are generally dangerous. However, the general interest can legitimize such an approach: environmental issues are, like road safety, such that for the common good they require everyone to modify their behavior as soon as it is harmful to the community, under penalty of severe sanctions. Provided it is ethically acceptable to design and implement a value policy, is it practically feasible?

To change environmental attitudes, one may want to resort to "ecological terror": fear is supposed to be a powerful driving force for action. In reality, fear probably paralyzes more than it encourages action: the more people believe that the end of the world is near, that disasters are inevitable and that no effective solutions exist to mitigate them, the more it is likely that irresponsible behaviors will develop rather than recede. Another solution might be to spread "ecological virtue" in society, through guilt or altruism, but both strategies look like uncertain bets on human nature and the power of public authorities.

The conviction that I express in this book is that there is a principle that is both fundamental and simple for changing environmental attitudes: the principle of justice.

The idea that ecological arguments are only understandable, particularly by "decision makers," when formulated in terms of economic efficiency ends up being worrying and quite unflattering for the decision makers in question. It is above all false. Our first aspiration in the social world is not efficiency but justice. The laws of nature, the Darwinian laws of natural selection and adaptation, are already laws of efficiency. Our added value in environmental debates consists of framing the complex problems that confront us in terms of justice and injustice.

Moreover, representing the ecological transition as an effort by public authorities to overcome the resistance of a civil society focused on its particular interests and short-sighted horizons is based on a threefold error. First, the ecological transition has become a priority for many in many different countries. It is now a matter of reconciling it with other priorities. Then, public power is not a benevolent force that constantly cares about the common good with a long-term perspective; nor is it an irresistible force. Economic interests and, more generally the forces of non-transition have captured entire sections of public action to neutralize them and prevent them from taking part in the transition. Even if public powers were to take action, they would have to deal with social complexity. The reinvention of forms of cooperation based on principles of justice principles within civil society, therefore, serves a dual purpose: to activate public authorities and their powerful institutional instruments (regulations, taxes, subsidies, etc.) and to guide them in this action.

The society we need to build is one where the response to global environmental change is social progress. Yes, transitions are possible: many highly resisted transitions in human history have eventually happened, including recently (abolition of slavery, emancipation of women, same-sex marriage). But they cannot happen, take hold, and accelerate without justice. This is ultimately the meaning of just transitions: transitions made possible by justice.

References

Agarwal, B., (2009), "Gender and forest conservation: The impact of women's participation in community forest governance", Ecological Economics, *68*(11), 2785–2799.

Association négaWatt, (2018), Energy sufficiency: Towards a more sustainable and fair society, 2018 https://negawatt.org/IMG/pdf/181029_energy-sufficiency_negawatt-scenario_eng.pdf

Agarwal, B., (2016), Gender Challenges (3 vol.), Oxford University Press, Oxford.

Andersson, J. and Atkinson, G., (2020), The distributional effects of a carbon tax: The role of income inequality. Centre for Climate Change Economics and Policy Working Paper 378/Grantham Research Institute on Climate Change and the Environment Working Paper 349, London, London School of Economics and Political Science.

Arnim, Scheidel et al., (2023), "Global impacts of extractive and industrial development projects on Indigenous Peoples' lifeways, lands, and rights." *Sci. Adv.* 9,eade9557.

Bar-On, Y. M., Phillips, R. and Milo, R., (2018) "The biomass distribution on Earth," *Proc Natl Acad Sci U S A*. 115(25):6506–6511.

Bernd, Bonfert (2024), "We like sharing energy but currently there's no advantage": Transformative opportunities and challenges of local energy communities in Europe, Energy Research & Social Science, 107.

Berry, A. and Laurent E., "Taxe carbone, le retour, à quelles conditions?", Working Paper de l'OFCE, n° 6, avril 2019.

Berlingieri, F., Colagrossi, M. and Mauri, C., (2023) Loneliness and social connectedness: insights from a new EU-wide survey, European Commission, 2023, JRC.

Blehaut, M., Gressier, M. (2023, Mai). En forte hausse, la précarité alimentaire s'ajoute à d'autres fragilités. Consommation et modes de vie, (329).

Bonneuil, C., Choquet, P.-L. and Franta, B., (2021), "Early warnings and emerging accountability: Total's responses to global warming, 1971–2021", Global Environmental Change, 71.

Bookchin, M., "Ecology and revolutionary thought" [1964], Post-Scarcity Anarchism, Ramparts Press, Palo Alto, 1971.

Bookchin, M., "Society and Ecology", (1993), on line. https://theanarchistlibrary.org/library/murray-bookchin-society-and-ecology.

Bourgeois, C., Giraudet L.-G. G. and Quirion P., (2019) Social-environmental-economic trade-offs associated with carbon-tax revenue recycling.

Boyce, J. K., (1994), "Inequality as a cause of environmental degradation", Ecological Economics, 11, (3), p. 169–178.
Boyce, J. K., (2002), The Political Economy of the Environment, Edward Elgar Publishing, Cheltenham, UK and Northampton, US.
Brand-Correa, L., Mattioli, G., Lamb, W. and Steinberger J. (2020), Understanding (and tackling) need satisfier escalation, Sustainability: Science, Practice and Policy, 16:1, 309–325. https://doi.org/10.1080/15487733.2020.1816026
Büchs, M. and Koch, M. (2017), Postgrowth and Wellbeing: Challenges to Sustainable Welfare, Basingstoke: Palgrave Macmillan.
Burke, Matthew (2022), "Post-growth Policies for the Future of Just Transitions in an Era of Uncertainty", 136 Futures.
Cassiers, I., Maréchal, K., & Méda, D. (Eds.). (2017). Post-growth Economics and Society: Exploring the Paths of a Social and Ecological Transition (1st ed.). Routledge.
CBD (2022), Kunming-Montreal Global Biodiversity Framework, 18 Dec. 2022, CBD/COP/15/L.25.
Chancel, L. (2022), Global carbon inequality over 1990–2019. Nat Sustain 5, 931–938. https://doi.org/10.1038/s41893-022-00955-z
Chancel, L., Piketty, T., Saez, E., Zucman, G. et al. (2022), World Inequality Report, World Inequality Lab.
CLEVER (2023), CLEVER: A Collaborative Low Energy Vision for the European Region, Climate neutrality, Energy security and Sustainability: A pathway to bridge the gap through Sufficiency, Efficiency and Renewables, final Report, June.
Creutzig, F., Niamir, L., Bai, X. et al. (2022), "Demand-side solutions to climate change mitigation consistent with high levels of well-being", *Nat. Clim. Chang.* 12, 36–46.
Celermajer, D., Schlosberg, D., Rickards, L., Stewart-Harawira, M., Thaler, M., Tschakert, P., Winter, C. (2020). "Multispecies justice: theories, challenges, and a research agenda for environmental politics", *Environmental Politics, 30*(1–2), 119–140.
Conseil national de l'alimentation or CNA (2022), "Prévenir et lutter contre la précarité alimentaire", Avis, n° 91, 19 octobre.
Dahlgren, G., & Whitehead, M. (1991). *Policies and Strategies to Promote Social Equity in Health*. Institute for Futures Studies.
Darimont, C. T., Cooke R., Bourbonnais M. L. et al., (2023), Humanity's diverse predatory niche and its ecological consequences, Commun Biol 6, 609.
Davis, O. and Baumberg Geiger, B. (2017), Did Food Insecurity Rise Across Europe After the 2008 Crisis? An analysis across welfare regimes, Social Policy and Society 16 (3): 343–36.
Dawson, N. M. et al., (2021), "The role of Indigenous peoples and local communities in effective and equitable conservation", *Ecology and Society*, 26(3), art. 19.
Deaton, Angus, (2013), The Great Escape: Health, Wealth, and the Origins of Inequality, Princeton (N. J.), Princeton University Press.
Dechezlepretre, A. et al., (2022a), "Les Français et les politiques climatiques", Les Notes du Conseil d'analyse économique, 73. .

Dechezlepretre, A. et al., (2022b), "Fighting climate change: International attitudes toward climate policies", OECD Economics Department Working Papers, No. 1714, OECD Publishing, Paris.

Del Bene, D. and Ávila S. (2023), Critical Mapping for Researching and Acting Upon Environmental Conflicts – The Case of the EJAtlas. In: Villamayor-Tomas S. and Muradian R. (eds.), The Barcelona School of Ecological Economics and Political Ecology. Studies in Ecological Economics, vol 8. Springer, Cham.

Douenne, T., (2018), The vertical and horizontal distributive effects of energy taxes, Policy Papers 2018.05, FAERE – French Association of Environmental and Resource Economists.

DWS (2019), The National Water and Sanitation Master Plan, South African Government.

Eaubonne F. D., (1974), Le Féminisme ou la mort, Horay, Paris.

Easterly, W. (1999), "Life During Growth." Journal of Economic Growth 4(3): 239–76.

Eckstein, David, Künzel, Vera, Schäfer,Laura and Winges, Maik. (2020), The Global Climate Risk Index 2020 – Who Suffers Most from Extreme Weather Events? Weather-Related Loss Events in 2018 and 1999 to 2018.

Eisenberg, A. (2019), "Just Transitions", Southern California Law Review, 92(2): 273–330.

Elhacham E., Ben-Uri L., Grozovski J. et al., (2020), "Global human-made mass exceeds all living biomass", *Nature*, vol. 588, p. 442–444.

Enqvist, J. P. and Ziervogel, G. (2019), Water governance and justice in Cape Town: An overview, WIREs Water 6:e1354.

ETUC (2016), Industrial Regions and Climate Policies: Towards a Just Transition., retrieved from ETUC.

Eurofound and the European Environment Agency (2021), Exploring the social challenges of low-carbon energy policies in Europe, Publications Office of the European Union, Luxembourg

European Commission. (2009), Communication from the Commission GDP and Beyond : Measuring Progress in a Changing World COM, 0433 Final.

European Commission (2019), The European Green Deal, Communication, COM, 640 final, 11 December. https://ec.europa.eu/info/sites/info/files/european-green-dealcommunication_en.pdf

European Commission (2023a), Fairness, inequality, and intergenerational mobility, Special Eurobarometer 529 Report.

European Commission (2023b). Fairness perceptions of the green transition, Special Eurobarometer 527 Report. Brussels: European Union.

European Environment Agency (2019), *Unequal Exposure and Unequal Impacts. Social Vulnerability to Air Pollution, Noise and Extreme Temperature in Europe*, Publications Office, Luxembourg.

European Environment Agency (2021), Economic losses and fatalities from weather- and climate-related events in Europe, Briefing no. 21/2021.

European Parliament. Directorate General for Parliamentary Research Services. (2023). *Beyond growth: Pathways towards sustainable prosperity in the EU*. Publications Office. https://data.europa.eu/doi/10.2861/602232

Eurostat (2018), Living conditions in Europe. Luxembourg: Publications Office of the European Union.

Fa, J. E. et al., (2020),"Importance of Indigenous peoples'lands for the conservation of Intact forest landscapes", *Frontiers in Ecology and the Environment*, 18(3), 135–140.

FAO, IFAD, UNICEF, WFP and WHO (2023), The State of Food Security and Nutrition in the World 2023. Urbanization, agrifood systems transformation and healthy diets across the rural–urban continuum, Rome, FAO.

FAO (2021), Alliance of Bioversity International et CIAT, *Indigenous Peoples' Food Systems. Insights on Sustainability and Resilience from the Front Line of Climate Change*, rapport, Rome.

Fabre, A., (2021), "Who are the citizens of the French Convention for Climate ?", HAL.

Farmer, P. (1999), *Infections and inequalities: The modern plagues* (1st ed.). University of California Press.

Fioramonti, L., Coscieme, L., Costanza, R., Kubiszewski, I., Trebeck, K., Wallis, S., ... & De Vogli, R. (2022). Wellbeing economy: An effective paradigm to mainstream post-growth policies? Ecological Economics, 192, 107261.

Flores, B. M., Montoya, E., Sakschewski, B. et al., (2024), Critical transitions in the Amazon forest system, Nature 626, 555–564.

Fondation de l'écologie politique, (2023), L'écologie depuis les ronds-points.

Fondation Zoein (2023), Étude pour le développement d'un projet pilote de revenu de transition écologique (RTE) dans le canton de Vaud.

Foster, J. B. (1999), Marx's Theory of Metabolic Rift: Classical foundations for environmental sociology, American Journal of Sociology, 105(2): 366–405.

Foster, J. B., (2000), Marx's Ecology, Monthly Review Press, New York.

Fransolet A. and Vanhille J. (eds.) (2023), Just Transition in Belgium: Concepts, issues at stake, and policy levers, Scientific report on behalf of the High Committee for a Just Transition, Brussels: November 2023.

Fransolet, A., and Laurent, E. (2024), *Mapping and Institutionalizing Social-Ecological Inequalities for a Just Transition in Europe* (SET papers No.1). Sciences Po, forthcoming.

Fressoz, Jean-Baptiste (2024), Sans transition – Une nouvelle histoire de l'énergie, Seuil.

Giraudet L.-G. et al., (2020), "Deliberating on climate action : insights from the French Citizens' Convention for Climate", HAL, 7 octobre.

Gough, Ian (2023), Sufficiency as a Value Standard: From Preferences to Needs, Ethics, Policy & Environment.

Greenpeace (2023), Viabilidad técnica y económica de un abono único de transporte en todo el Estado español.

Grossman M., (1972),"On the Concept of Health Capital and the Demand for Health", Journal of Political Economy,80(2), 223–255.

Grove, R. H., (1995), Green Imperialism. Colonial Expansion, Tropical Island Edens and the Origins of Environmentalism, 1600–1860, Cambridge University Press, Cambridge.

Grove, R. H., (2018), "Science coloniale et naissance de l'écologie", Écologie & politique, 56(1), 83–102.

Gupta J., et al. (2023), Earth system justice needed to identify and live within Earth system boundaries, Nature Sustainability 6: 630–638.
Ghebreyesus, T. A. (2023). "Achieving health for all requires action on the economic and commercial determinants of health", The Lancet, 401(10383), 1137–1139. https://doi.org/10.1016/S0140-6736(23)00574-3
Hardin, Garrett, (1968), "The Tragedy of the Commons", Science, 162(3859): 1243–48. http://www.jstor.org/stable/1724745.
Hensher, M., Canny, B., Zimitat., C., Campbell, J., and Palmer A. (2020), "Health care, overconsumption and uneconomic growth: a conceptual framework", Soc Sci Med. 266113420.
Hickel, J., (2021), "The anti-colonial politics of degrowth", Political Geography, 88.
High-Level Commission on Health Employment and Economic Growth (2016), Working for health and growth: investing in the health workforce. Report of the High-Level Commission on Health Employment and Economic Growth, World Health Organization.
Hirvilammi, Tuuli (2020), "The Virtuous Circle of Sustainable Welfare as a Transformative Policy Idea", Sustainability 12(1): 391. https://doi.org/10.3390/su12010391
Hopkins, Rob (2008), The Transition Handbook. From Oil Dependency to Local Resilience, Green books.
Holt-Lunstad, J., & Perissinotto, C. (2023), "Social Isolation and Loneliness as Medical Issues", New England Journal of Medicine, 388(3), 193–195. https://doi.org/10.1056/NEJMp2208029
Horton, Richard et al. (2015), "Planetary health a new science for exceptional action", The Lancet, 386(10007), 1921–1922.
ICCA Consortium (2021), Territories of Life Report, ICCA Consortium.
ILO (2015), Guidelines for a just transition towards environmentally sustainable economies and societies for all, Geneva, ILO.
IOC-UNESCO. (2024), State of the Ocean Report. Paris, IOC-UNESCO. (IOC Technical Series, 190).
International Labour Organiszation (ILO) and United Nations Environment Programme (UNEP) (2023), Just Transition Finance: Pathways for banking and insurance, Geneva.
IPBES (2019), Summary for Policymakers of the Global Assessment Report on Biodiversity and Ecosystem Services of the Intergovernmental Science-Policy Platform on Biodiversity and Ecosystem Services. S. Díaz, J. Settele, E. S. Brondízio, H. T. Ngo, M. Guèze, J. Agard, A. Arneth, P. Balvanera, K. A. Brauman, S. H. M. Butchart, K. M. A. Chan, L. A. Garibaldi, K. Ichii, J. Liu, S. M. Subramanian, G. F. Midgley, P. Miloslavich, Z. Molnár, D. Obura, A. Pfaff, S. Polasky, A. Purvis, J. Razzaque, B. Reyers, R. Roy Chowdhury, Y. J. Shin, I. J. VisserenHamakers, K. J. Willis and C. N. Zayas (eds.), IPBES secretariat, Bonn, Germany.
IPBES (2022), Methodological Assessment Report on the Diverse Values and Valuation of Nature of the Intergovernmental Science-Policy Platform on Biodiversity and Ecosystem Services. P. Balvanera, U. Pascual M. Christie,

B. Baptiste, and D. González-Jiménez (eds.), IPBES secretariat, Bonn, Germany. DOI: https://doi.org/10.5281/zenodo.6522522

IPBES (2022), Thematic Assessment Report on the Sustainable Use of Wild Species of the Intergovernmental Science-Policy Platform on Biodiversity and Ecosystem Services. J.M. Fromentin, M. R. Emery, J. Donaldson, M. C. Danner, A. Hallosserie, and D. Kieling (eds.), IPBES secretariat, Bonn, Germany.

IPCC (2022), Climate Change 2022: Impacts, Adaptation, and Vulnerability. Contribution of Working Group II to the Sixth Assessment Report of the Intergovernmental Panel on Climate Change. H.-O. Pörtner, D. C. Roberts, M. Tignor, E. S. Poloczanska, K. Mintenbeck, A. Alegría, M. Craig, S. Langsdorf, S. Löschke, V. Möller, A. Okem, B. Rama (eds.), Cambridge University Press.

IPCC (2023), AR6 Synthesis Report: Climate Change 2023 https://www.ipcc.ch/report/ar6/syr/

Ipsos | BNP Paribas, (2023), Just Transition, April.

Jonas Lage, Johannes Thema, Carina Zell-Ziegler, Benjamin Best, Luisa Cordroch and Frauke Wiese, (2023), Citizens call for sufficiency and regulation — A comparison of European citizen assemblies and National Energy and Climate Plans, Energy Research & Social Science, 104.

Just Transition Research Collaborative (JTRC) (2018), Mapping Just Transitions to a Low Carbon World.

King Y., (1983), "The ecology of feminism and the feminism of ecology", in Plant J., Healing the Wounds. The Promise of Ecofeminism, New Society Publishers, Philadelphie, p. 18–28.

Kickbusch, I., Allen, L., and Franz, C. (2016), The commercial determinants of health. The Lancet Global Health, 4(12), e895–e896. https://doi.org/10.1016/S2214-109X(16)30217-0

Kukowski C. A. and Garnett E. E., (2023), Tackling inequality is essential for behaviour change for net zero, Nat. Clim. Chang.

Lage, Jonas, Johannes Thema, Carina Zell-Ziegler, Benjamin Best, Luisa Cordroch and Frauke Wiese (2023), Citizens call for sufficiency and regulation — A comparison of European citizen assemblies and National Energy and Climate Plans, Energy Research & Social Science, 104.

La Gioia Adriano, Fransolet Aurore, Hudon Marek and Sandrine Meyer (2023), "Just Transition" Visions: An analysis of the perception of the Belgian actors, Working paper.

Lakeman S., (2024), Emerging local energy communities, Nat Energy 9: 9.

Landemore H. (2020), Open Democracy: Reinventing popular rule for the twenty-first century, Princeton University Press.

Larrère C. (2012), "L'écoféminisme: féminisme écologique ou écologie féministe", Tracés, Revue de sciences humaines, n° 22.

Laurent, Éloi, (2018), Measuring Tomorrow: Accounting for Well-Being, Resilience, and Sustainability in the Twenty-First Century. Princeton University Press.

Laurent, É. (2024), Sufficiency as a confluence for post-growth streams—Report on the integrated analysis of the different schools of thought. *Zenodo.* https://doi.org/10.5281/ZENODO.13682536

Laurent É. (2023), Économie pour le XXIe siècle: Manuel des transitions justes. La Découverte.

Laurent É. and Zwickl K. (eds.) (2021), The Routledge Handbook of the Political Economy of the Environment (1st ed.), Routledge.

Leopold, L. (1995), Presentation, Our Lakes, Our Health, Our Future. Proceedings of the International Joint Commission's 1995 Biennial Meeting on Great Lakes Water Quality, September 22-25,Duluth, Minnesota, pp. 80–82.

Lepenies, P. (2016), The Power of a Single Number: A Political History of GDP. Columbia University Press.

Link, B. G., and Phelan, J. (1995), Social conditions as fundamental causes of disease. Journal of Health and Social Behavior, Spec No, 80–94.

Marianne Bléhaut and Mathilde Gressier (2023), "En forte hausse, la précarité alimentaire s'ajoute à d'autres fragilités", Etude du CREDOC 329, mai.

Marks D.and Connell, J. (2023), Unequal and unjust: The political ecology of Bangkok's increasing urban heat island, Urban Studies.

Marmot M., (2010), Fair Society, Healthy Lives : A Strategic Review of Health Inequalities in England Post-2010, The Institute of Health Equity.

Marmot, M. (2018), Inclusion health: Addressing the causes of the causes. *The Lancet*, *391*(10117), 186–188. https://doi.org/10.1016/S0140-6736(17)32848-9

Marmot, M. (2020), Health equity in England: The Marmot review 10 years on. *BMJ*, m693. https://doi.org/10.1136/bmj.m693

Martinez-Alier J. (2002), The Environmentalism of the poor: A study of ecological conflicts and valuation, Edward Elgar Publishing, Cheltenham, UK and Northampton, US.

Martinez-Alier J. and M. O'Connor (1999), Distributional Issues: An overview. In Handbook of Environmental and Resource Economics, edited by J. van den Bergh, p. 380–392, Edward Elgar Publishing, Cheltenham, UK and Northampton, US

Martinez, R., Lloyd-Sherlock, P., Soliz, P., Ebrahim, S., Vega, E., Ordunez, P., & McKee, M. (2020), Trends in premature avertable mortality from non-communicable diseases for 195 countries and territories, 1990–2017: A population-based study. *The Lancet Global Health*, *8*(4), e511–e523. https://doi.org/10.1016/S2214-109X(20)30035-8

Martire, S, Castellani, V. and Sala, S. (2015), Carrying capacity assessment of forest resources: Enhancing environmental sustainability in energy production at local scale, Resour. Conserv. Recycl., 9411–20, 10.1016/j.resconrec.2014.11.002

Marx, Karl (1976), Capital (vol.1), London: Penguin.

Mazzochi, Tony, (1993), "A Superfund for Workers", Earth Island 9(1)p. 40–41.

Mehleb R. I., Kallis G. and Zografos C., "A discourse analysis of yellow-vest resistance against carbon taxes", Environmental Innovation and Societal Transitions, vol. 40, 2021, p. 382–394.

Merchant C., *The Death of Nature*. Harper & Row, New York, 1980.

Modi, Neena (2022) Valuing Health - Why prioritising population health is essential to prosperity, British Medical Association.

Mokbul Ahmad Morshed, Hayatullah Mushwani, Kawoon Sahak and Mohammad Haroon Hairan, The current state of early warning system in South Asia: A case study of Afghanistan, International Journal of Disaster Risk Reduction, Volume 100, 2024, 104201, ISSN 2212–4209, https://doi.org/10.1016/j.ijdrr.2023.104201.

Moore J. W., Capitalism in the Web of Life, (2015), Ecology and the Accumulation of Capital, Verso, New York.

Morena E., D. Krause, D. Stevis (eds.), (2019), Just Transitions: Social Justice in the Shift towards a Low-Carbon World, Pluto Press, London.

Morel, P. (2020). Distinguer sans séparer. La définition aristotélicienne de la vertu éthique. Revue de philosophie ancienne, XXXVIII, 187–213.

Mokbul Ahmad Morshed, Hayatullah Mushwani, Kawoon Sahak, Mohammad Haroon Hairan (2024),"The current state of early warning system in South Asia: A case study of Afghanistan", International Journal of Disaster Risk Reduction, 100.

Musgrave R. A. (1959), The Theory of Public Finance, McGraw Hill, New York.

Narayan S., (2023), Just Transition for Healthy People on a Healthy Planet, NEW SOLUTIONS: A Journal of Environmental and Occupational Health Policy, 33(1):72–82.

Nature (2023), "The science is clear: sustainable development and climate action are inseparable", Nature 620, 921–922.

Nayak, P.K., Pradhan, S.K. (2023). Interdisciplinary Perspectives on Social-ecological Wellbeing. In: Chetri, S., Dutta, T., Mandal, M.K., Patnaik, P. (eds) Handbook of Happiness. Springer, Singapore.

New Zealand Ministry of Justice (2017), Te Awa Tupua (Whanganui River Claims Settlement) Act 2017, Wellington: Parliamentary Counsel Office.

Nhamo, G. and Agyepong, A. O. (2019), Climate change adaptation and local government: Institutional complexities surrounding Cape Town's Day Zero, Jamba J. Disaster Risk Stud. 11:717.

OECD (2011), *Towards Green Growth*, OECD Green Growth Studies, OECD Publishing, Paris, https://doi.org/10.1787/9789264111318-en.

Office of the Surgeon General. (2023). *Our Epidemic of Loneliness and Isolation: The Surgeon General's Advisory on the Healing Effects of Social Connection and Community.*

One Health High-Level Expert Panel (OHHLEP), Adisasmito W. B., Almuhairi S., Behravesh C. B., Bilivogui P. et al. (2022), One Health: A new definition for a sustainable and healthy future, PLOS Pathogens 18 (6): e1010537.

Ostrom E., (1990), Governing the Commons. The Evolution of Institutions for Collective Actions, Cambridge University Press, Cambridge.

Ostrom, Elinor (2024), Biographical. NobelPrize.org. Nobel Prize Outreach AB 2024. Wed. 3 Jan 2024.

Ostrom, Elinor (2010), Beyond Markets and States: Polycentric Governance of Complex Economic Systems, American Economic Review, 100 (3): 641–72.

Ostrom, Elinor, (2009), "A general framework for analyzing sustainability of social-ecological systems", Science, 325, p. 419.

Oxford English Dictionary (2016), reference, v. 3. Oxford: Oxford University.

Pascual U., Balvanera P., Anderson C. B. et al., (2023), Diverse values of nature for sustainability", Nature 620, p. 813–823.

Paulsson, A., Koch, M. & Fritz, M., (2024) Diminishing returns of growth? Economic performance, needs satisfaction and ecological impacts of OECD welfare states, Critical Social Policy.

Persson L, Carney Almroth BM, Collins CD, Cornell S, de Wit CA, Diamond ML, Fantke P, Hassellöv M, MacLeod M, Ryberg MW, Søgaard Jørgensen P, Villarrubia-Gómez P, Wang Z, Hauschild MZ. Outside the Safe Operating Space of the Planetary Boundary for Novel Entities. Environ Sci Technol. 2022 Feb 1;56(3):1510-1521. doi: 10.1021/acs.est.1c04158. Epub 2022 Jan 18. PMID: 35038861; PMCID: PMC8811958.

Petticrew, M., Glover, R. E., Volmink, J., Blanchard, L., Cott, É., Knai, C., Maani, N., Thomas, J., Tompson, A., Van Schalkwyk, M. C. I., and Welch, V. (2023), "The Commercial Determinants of Health and Evidence Synthesis (CODES): Methodological guidance for systematic reviews and other evidence syntheses", Systematic Reviews, 12(1), 165. https://doi.org/10.1186/s13643-023-02323-0

Pollin R. and Callaci, B. (2019), "The Economics of Just Transition: A Framework for Supporting Fossil Fuel–Dependent Workers and Communities in the United States," Labor Studies Journal, 44(2), 93–138.

Pollin, Robert N. (2023), "Fossil Fuel Industry Phase-Out and Just Transition: Designing Policies to Protect Workers' Living Standards", Journal of Human Development and Capabilities.

Pope Francis (2015), Encyclical Letter Laudato Si' of the Holy Father Francis On Care for Our Common Home, Our Sunday Visitor.

Preston S., (1975), "The changing relation between mortality and level of economic development", 29, pp. 231–48 (Reprinted Int J Epidemiol)

Pritchett L. and Summers L. H., (1996), "Wealthier is healthier", J Hum Resources, 31, pp. 841–68.

Rockström J., Gupta J., Qin D. et al. (2023), Safe and just Earth system boundaries, Nature 619, 102–111.

Rogers A. D. and d'A. D. Laffoley (2011), International Earth system expert workshop on ocean stresses and impacts, Summary report, IPSO, Oxford.

Savelli E., Mazzoleni, M., Di Baldassarre, G. et al. (2023), Urban water crises driven by elites' unsustainable consumption. Nat Sustain 6, 929–940.

Shiva V., Staying Alive. (1988), Women, Ecology and Survival in India, Kali for Women, New Delhi.

Schlosberg D. and Carruthers D., (2010), "Indigenous struggles, environmental justice, and community capabilities", *Global Environmental Politics*, 10(4), 12–35.

Singh, G. and Hickel, J. (2023), Capitalogenic disease: Social determinants in focus. BMJ Global Health, 8(12), e013661. https://doi.org/10.1136/bmjgh-2023-013661

Steyn, G., Tyler, E., Rof,f A., Renaud, C. and Mgoduso, L. (2021), "The Just Transition Transaction: A Developing Country Coal Power Retirement Mechanism", Meridian Economics, Cape Town, South Africa.

Steffen, W., Richardson, K., Rockström, J., Cornell, S. E., Fetzer, I., Bennett, E. M., Biggs, R., Carpenter, S. R., de Vries W., de Wit C. A., Folke, C., Gerten, D., Heinke, J., Mace, G. M., Persson, L. M., Ramanathan, V., Reyers, B., and Sörlin, S. (2015), "Sustainability. Planetary boundaries: guiding human development on a changing planet", Science. 2015 Feb 13;347(6223):1259855. doi:10.1126/science.1259855. PMID: 25592418.

Stegeman, Ingrid, Vania Putatti, Alba Godfrey, and Caroline Costongs (2024), "Strengthening the European Semester to Achieve Economies of Wellbeing", International Journal of Environmental Research and Public Health, 21, 5(634). https://doi.org/10.3390/ijerph21050634

Stone, Christopher (1972), "Should Trees Have Standing? – Towards Legal. Rights for Natural Objects", Southern California Law Review 45, (1972): 450–501.

Swaton S. (2018), Pour un revenu de transition écologique, Presses Universitaires de France.

The COP24 (2018) declaration, "Solidarity and Just Transition: Silesia Declaration", Warsaw, Ministry of the Environment.

The World Bank Group and the Asian Development Bank (2021), Climate Risk Country Profile: Thailand.

Thomas A. (2021), Framing the just transition: How international trade unions engage with UN climate negotiations, Global Environmental Change, 70, Article 102347. https://doi.org/10.1016/j.gloenvcha.2021.102347.

Theil, Henri and Finke, Renate (1983), "The distance from the equator as an instrumental variable," Economics Letters, Elsevier, 13(4), 357–360.

Titmuss R. M. (1983), Social Policy. An Introduction. Brian Abel-Smith and Kay Titmuss (eds), London: George Allen & Unwin.

UNDP (United Nations Development Programme) Human Development Report Office (2010), Human Development Report. The Real Wealth of Nations: Pathways to Human Development. New York.

UNDP (2022), "How Just Transition Can Help Deliver the Paris Agreement", United Nations, Geneva.

UNFCCC (2023), Conference of the Parties serving as the meeting of the Parties to the Paris Agreement, Fifth session, First global stocktake, 13 December.

United Nations Environment Programme (2021), Understanding the State of the Ocean: A Global Manual on Measuring SDG 14.1.1, SDG 14.2.1 and SDG 14.5.1. Nairobi.

United Nations Office for Disaster Risk Reduction and World Meteorological Organization (2023), Global Status of Multi-Hazard Early Warning Systems. Geneva, Switzerland.

Villamayor-Tomas, Sergio and Roldan Muradian (eds.), (2023), The Barcelona School of Ecological Economics and Political Ecology: A Companion in Honour of Joan Martinez-Alier, Cham: Springer.

Waldinger, Robert and Marc Schulz (2023), The Good Life, Simon and Schuster.

Walzer M., (1983), Spheres of Justice. A Defense of Pluralism and Equality, Basic Books, New York.

Wang G., Macera C. A., Scudder-Soucie B., Schmid T., Pratt M. and Buchner D. (2005), A cost-benefit analysis of physical activity using bike/pedestrian trails, Health Promotion Practice, 6 (2), 174–179, https://doi.org/10.1177/1524839903260687

White, L. (1967), "The Historical Roots of Our Ecologic Crisis", Science, 155(3767), 1203–1207.

Wierling, A., Schwanitz, V.J., Zeiss, J.P. et al. (2023), A Europe-wide inventory of citizen-led energy action with data from 29 countries and over 10000 initiatives. Sci Data 10(9), https://doi.org/10.1038/s41597-022-01902-5

Ripple, WJ et al. (2024), An environmental and socially just climate mitigation pathway for a planet in peril, Environ. Res. Lett. 19 021001.

Wilkinson, R. G., and Pickett, K. E. (2006). Income inequality and population health: A review and explanation of the evidence. *Social Science & Medicine*, *62*(7), 1768–1784. https://doi.org/10.1016/j.socscimed.2005.08.036

WHO Council on the Economics of Health for All (2023). Health for All – transforming economies to deliver what matters: final report of the WHO Council on the Economics of Health for All. Geneva: World Health Organization.

WMO (2023), WMO-No. 1316, State of the Global Climate 2022.

Ziervogel G. (2019), Understanding the Cape Town Drought: Lessons Learned, https://www.africancentreforcities.net/wp-content/uploads/2019/02/Ziervogel-2019-Lessons-from-Cape-Town-Drought_A.pdf.

Index